365

WAYS TO FIND

PEACE

EDITED BY
MARCUS BRAYBROOKE

365
WAYS TO FIND
PEACE

MEDITATIONS & INSPIRATIONS

WATKINS
Sharing Wisdom Since 1893

365 Ways to Find Peace
General Editor: Marcus Braybrooke

First published as *365 Meditations and Inspirations on Love and Peace* in the United Kingdom and Ireland in 2002. This revised edition published in 2019 by
Watkins, an imprint of Watkins Media Limited
Unit 11, Shepperton House
89–93 Shepperton Road
London N1 3DF

enquiries@watkinspublishing.com

British Library Cataloguing-in-Publication Data:
A catalogue record for this book is available from the British Library

10 9 8 7 6 5 4 3 2 1

ISBN 978-1-78678-215-1

Typeset in Cera Pro and Cardenio Modern
Printed and bound in China

NOTES: Abbreviations used throughout this book:
CE Common Era (the equivalent of AD)
BCE Before the Common Era (the equivalent of BC)
b. born, d. died

158. 128
Thr

CONTENTS

INTRODUCTION BY MARCUS BRAYBROOKE   VII

THE CENTRE OF BEING   1
True self   4
Self-esteem   8
Inner strength   10
Stillness   16
Inner wisdom   21
Giving   26
Thankfulness   30
Wonder   32
Being in time   38
Attentiveness   47
Nature   49
Acceptance   50
Simplicity   54
Happiness   57
Truth   60
Wordlessness   63
Humility   66
Faith   69

THE INNER CIRCLE OF LOVE   76
Empathy   78

Selflessness   81
Compassion   83
Friendship   89
Family   94
Karma   99
Everyday love   103
Sacred union   111
Mystic love   116
Partings   122
New Life   124

THE OUTER CIRCLE OF SPIRIT   132

In times of darkness   134
The way   143
A world of kinship   157
A world of harmony   164
A world of peace   176
The one   179
Near and far horizons   190
Eternity   204

ACKNOWLEDGEMENTS   207

INTRODUCTION

However storm-tossed our life's voyage might seem
to us, there is always, in the depths of our inner being,
a source of calm – if we only know how to find it. But
amidst all the turbulence of our emotions and anxieties,
and amidst the pressures of our worldly responsibilities,
where do we even start to look?

Through the centuries many writers, astonishingly
different in their personal circumstances and their
beliefs, as well as in their social and historical settings,
have succeeded somehow in putting into words
profound thoughts that persuade us of certain universal
truths and values. These ideas cut across distinctions
of race, class, gender, age and religion. Some of
the most inspiring of these writings are those that
concentrate on peace, love and the spirit – for these
are the things that really matter in life, whatever our
faith and whatever our politics. These are the essentials
that provide a foundation for living more at ease with
ourselves, with each other, with whatever life brings us,
and with the certainty of our mortality.

All the inspirations quoted in this book are reminders
of the deep stillness and tranquillity we can find in a life
of acceptance, simplicity, compassion, thankfulness,
love and faith. In making contact with this stillness
at the core of ourselves, we are touched by a power

greater than our own. We can all draw strength, hope and renewal from this inexhaustible well of blessings.

If we detach ourselves from the distractions that oppress the spirit, all the energy previously absorbed in inner turmoil is set free to flow in love, for ourselves, our friends and our loved ones, all the people around us, all those who are suffering, even those who wish us harm – indeed the whole of humanity with whom we share a precious spiritual kinship.

Love and compassion can help us counter the conflict and violence within and between nations. Each of us can become a beacon of peace, radiating healing light into the world. Love for ourselves may seem at first rather self-centred, but self-love or self-respect is a vital foundation for love extended to others, and so sets the theme of the first section of this book, "The Centre of Being". From here the focus gradually spirals outward, through "The Inner Circle of Love" (covering such vital topics as compassion, karma, friendship, family) to "The Outer Circle of Spirit" – our relationship with the world at large and with the One within and beyond.

Read, reflect, and be inspired – if you find wisdom here, carry it with you, and enjoy its gifts to the full.

Marcus Braybrooke

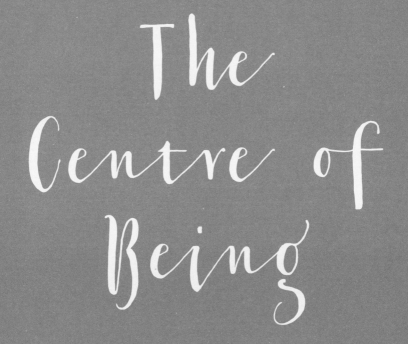

The
Centre of
Being

TRUE SELF
001...008

SELF-ESTEEM
009...012

INNER STRENGTH
013...024

STILLNESS
025...034

INNER WISDOM
035...046

GIVING
047...054

THANKFULNESS
055...058

WONDER
059...069

BEING IN TIME
070...086

ATTENTIVENESS
087...089

NATURE
090...092

ACCEPTANCE
093...100

SIMPLICITY
101...106

HAPPINESS
107...112

TRUTH
113...118

WORDLESSNESS
119...123

HUMILITY
124...129

FAITH
130...143

TRUE SELF

001. OPENING THE SELF

The door to the human heart can be opened
only from the inside.
Spanish proverb

002. ME MYSELF

Trippers and askers surround me,
People I meet, the effect upon me of my early life
or the ward and
   city I live in, or the nation,
The latest dates, discoveries, inventions, societies,
authors old
   and new ...
These come to me days and nights and go from me
again,
But they are not the Me myself.
Walt Whitman (1819–92), from "Song of Myself",
USA

003. TEA AT THE PALAZ OF HOON

Not less because in purple I descended
The western day through what you called
The loneliest air, not less was I myself.

What was the ointment sprinkled on my beard?
What were the hymns that buzzed beside my ears?
What was the sea whose tide swept through me
there?

Out of my mind the golden ointment rained,
And my ears made the blowing hymns they heard.
I was myself the compass of that sea:

I was the world in which I walked, and what I saw
Or heard or felt came not but from myself;
And there I found myself more truly and more
strange.
Wallace Stevens (1879–1955), USA

004. LUTE MUSIC

My soul gave me good counsel, teaching me that the lamp which I carry does not belong to me, and the song that I sing was not generated from within me. Even if I walk with light, I am not the light; and if I am a taut-stringed lute, I am not the lute-player.
Jalal al-Din Rumi (1207–73), Persia

005. A FREE MIND

A free mind is one which is untroubled and unfettered by anything, which has not bound its best part to any particular manner of being or worship and which does not seek its own interest in anything but is always immersed in God's most precious will ... There is no work which men and women can perform, however small, which does not draw from this its power and strength.
Meister Eckhart (1260–1328), Germany

006. SELF-KNOWLEDGE

This is the miracle of life: that each person who heeds himself knows what no scientist can ever know: who he is.

Søren Kierkegaard (1813–55), Denmark

007. WITHIN THE CIRCLE OF SELF

Two exercises at life's beginning: to narrow the circle round about you more and more, and to check, again and again, that you are not hiding somewhere outside that circle.

Franz Kafka (1883–1924), Austria

008. MIRROR IMAGE

The Self exists both inside
and outside the physical body,
just as an image exists inside
and outside the mirror.

From the *Ashtavakra Gita* (c.200BCE–c.200CE), India

SELF-ESTEEM

009. A DROP IN THE OCEAN

We ourselves feel that what we are doing is just a drop in the ocean. But if that drop was not in the ocean, I think the ocean would be less because of that missing drop.

Mother Teresa of Calcutta (1910–97), India

010. THE GOLDEN ETERNITY

Remember the golden eternity is yourself.

Jack Kerouac (1922–69), USA

011. COMPASSION

If your compassion does not include yourself,
it is incomplete.
The Buddha (c.563–c.483BCE), India

012. LOOK WITHIN

If the eye were not sun-like, it could not see the
sun; if we did not carry within us the very power
of God, how could anything God-like delight us?
Johann Wolfgang von Goethe (1749–1832), Germany

INNER STRENGTH

013. RIDE ON SINGING

If you have a fearful thought, do not share it with someone who is weak: whisper it to your saddle-bow, and ride on singing.

King Alfred of Wessex (c.849–c.899), England

014. INTIMACY

I can be alone,
I know how to be alone.

There is a tacit understanding
between my pencils
and the trees outside;
between the rain
and my luminous hair.

The tea is boiling:
my golden zone,
my pure burning amber.

I can be alone,
I know how to be alone.
By tea-light
I write.

Nina Cassian (1924–2014), Romania

015. THE BREAKTHROUGH

And the day came when the risk
to remain tight in a bud was more
painful than the risk it took to blossom.
Anaïs Nin (1903–77), France

016. DESTINY

If you will not fight your battle of life because
in selfishness you are afraid of the battle, your
resolution is in vain: nature will compel you.
From the *Bhagavad Gita* (1st–2nd century BCE),
India

017. THE GIFT OF FORTITUDE

Nothing happens to any man which he is not formed
by nature to bear.
Marcus Aurelius (121–80), Rome

018. COMRADES IN CREATION

I am no more lonely than a single mullein or dandelion in a pasture, or a bean leaf, or sorrel, or a horse-fly, or a bumblebee. I am no more lonely than the Mill Brook, or a weathercock, or the north star, or the south wind, or an April shower, or a January thaw, or the first spider in a new house.

Henry David Thoreau (1817–62), USA

019. DIFFICULTIES

It is not because things are difficult that we do not dare; it is because we do not dare that they are difficult.

Seneca (c.4bce–c.65ce), Rome

020. THE SELF-RELIANT SOUL

The poise of a plant, the bended tree recovering itself from the strong wind, the vital resources of every vegetable and animal, are also demonstrations of the self-sufficing, and therefore self-relying soul. All history from its highest to its trivial passages is the various record of this power.
Ralph Waldo Emerson (1803–82), USA

021. A FAVOURABLE WIND

The wind of God's grace is incessantly blowing. Lazy sailors on the sea of life do not take advantage of it. But the active and the strong always keep the sails of their minds unfurled to catch the favourable wind and thus reach their destination very soon.
Mahatma Gandhi (1869–1948), India

022. GENTLE STRENGTH

Good doors have no bolts
    yet cannot be forced.
Good knots have no rope
    but cannot be untied.

Lao Tzu (c.604–c.531BCE), from the *Tao Te Ching*,
China

023. THE STORM OF FEAR

The wise man in the storm prays to God, not for
safety from danger, but for deliverance from fear.
It is the storm within that endangers him, not the
storm without.

Ralph Waldo Emerson (1803–82), USA

024. THE PLOT AGAINST THE GIANT

First Girl: When this yokel comes maundering,
Whetting his hacker,
I shall run before him,
Diffusing the civilest odors
Out of geraniums and unsmelled flowers.
It will check him.

Second Girl: I shall run before him,
Arching cloths besprinkled with colors
As small as fish-eggs.
The threads
Will abash him.

Third Girl: Oh, la . . . le pauvre!
I shall run before him,
With a curious puffing.
He will bend his ear then.
I shall whisper
Heavenly labials in a world of gutterals.
It will undo him.

Wallace Stevens (1879–1955), USA

STILLNESS

025. HERMITAGE AT BROKEN-HILL MONASTERY

Within this convent old
By the clear dawn
Tall woods are lit with earliest rays.
Lo here and there a pathway strays
On to a hidden lawn
Whose flowery thickets cells enfold.

The light upon yon hill
Lulls every bird;
And shadows on dark tarns set free
The souls of men from vanity.
Each sound of earth is still.
Only the temple bell is heard.
Ch'ang Chien (c.8th century), China

026. DIVINE STILLNESS

Nothing in all creation is so like God as stillness.
Meister Eckhart (1260–1328), Germany

027. THE SOUL IN THE GARDEN OF PEACE

Meanwhile the mind, from pleasure less,
Withdraws into its happiness;
The mind, that ocean where each kind
Does straight its own resemblance find;
Yet it creates, transcending these,
Far other worlds and other seas,
Annihilating all that's made
To a green thought in a green shade.

Here at the fountain's sliding foot,
Or at some fruit tree's mossy root,
Casting the body's vest aside,
My soul into the boughs does glide:
There, like a bird, it sits and sings,
Then whets and combs its silver wings,
And, till prepared for longer flight,
Waves in its plumes the various light.
Andrew Marvell (1621–78), from "The Garden",
England

028. HEAVEN-HAVEN

A nun takes the veil

I have desired to go
Where springs not fail,
To fields where flies no sharp and sided hail
And a few lilies blow.

And I have asked to be
Where no storms come,
Where the green swell is in the havens dumb,
And out of the swing of the sea.
Gerard Manley Hopkins (1844–89), England

029. REVELATION

To the mind that is still, the whole universe
surrenders.
Lao Tzu (c.604–c.531BCE), from the *Tao Te Ching*,
China

030. NO BOTHER

Zen meditation.
Blood-gorged
Mosquitoes.
Tan Taigi (1709–71), Japan

031. A QUIET MIND

You must strive for a quiet mind. If the
eyes are perpetually restless, they cannot
appreciate a beautiful object set before them;
they glance this way and that, and so fail to
discern the subtlety of the object's form and
colour. Equally, if the mind is perpetually restless,
distracted by a thousand worldly concerns,
it cannot apprehend the truth.
St Basil the Great (330–79), Turkey

032. THE GREAT TREE

Praise and blame, gain and loss, pleasure and
sorrow come and go like the wind. To be happy,
rest like a great tree in the midst of them all.
Achaan Chah (1918–92), Thailand

033. RETURN TO THE SOURCE

Empty yourself of everything.
Let your mind be at peace.
While ten thousand things rise and fall,
  the Self contemplates their return.
Each of them grows and flourishes and
  then returns to the source.
Returning to the source is stillness,
  which is the way of nature.
Lao Tzu (c.604–c.531BCE), from the *Tao Te Ching*,
China

034. ATTENTIVENESS

The no-mind state is not the vacancy of idiocy but
the most supremely alert intelligence, undistracted
by extraneous thought.
Ramesh Balsekar (1917–2009), India

INNER WISDOM

035. STARLIGHT

All men have stars ... but they are not the same things for different people. For some, who are travellers, the stars are guides. For others, they are no more than little lights in the sky. For others, who are scholars, they are problems. ... But all these stars are silent.

You – you alone – will have the stars as no one else has them.

Antoine de Saint-Exupéry (1900–44), France

036. THE MIND'S CONTRIBUTION

We must deliver ourselves with the help of our minds. ... for one who has conquered the mind, the mind is the best of friends; but for one who has failed to do so, the mind will remain the greatest enemy.

From the *Bhagavad Gita* (1st–2nd century BCE), India

037. KNOWLEDGE AND WISDOM

Knowledge comes, but wisdom lingers.
Alfred, Lord Tennyson (1809–92), England

038. THE VOICE OF CONSCIENCE

Conscience sometimes speaks with the voice of
society, sometimes with the voice of the heart.
Deep in ourselves we always know the difference.
Jeanne Tardiveau (1920–94), St Lucia

039. FREE WILL

I have given you words of vision and wisdom more
secret than hidden mysteries. Ponder them in the
silence of your soul, and then in freedom do your
will.
From the _Bhagavad Gita_ (1st–2nd century BCE), India

040. THE BALANCE OF BEING

You must learn to be still in the midst of activity and to be vibrantly alive in repose.
Mahatma Gandhi (1869–1948), India

041. PRIORITIES

You seek too much information and not enough transformation.
Shirdi Sai Baba (1838–1918), India

042. PEACE AND REASON

Withdraw into your inner self. The rational principle which rules there is content with itself when it acts justly, and so maintains its own tranquillity.

Marcus Aurelius (121–80), Rome

043. THE RULE OF THE INNER SELF

No one outside ourselves can rule us inwardly. When we know this, we become free.

The Buddha (c.563–c.483BCE), India

044. PATIENCE

The heart is cooking a pot of food for you.
Be patient until it is cooked.
Jalal al-Din Rumi (1207–73), Persia

045. THE SOURCE OF GOODNESS

Dig inside. Inside is the fountain of good,
and it will forever flow, if you will forever dig.
Marcus Aurelius (121–80), Rome

046. THE HEART'S MIRROR

Leave all worries behind and make your heart
totally pure, like the face of a mirror
with no image or design.
Once your heart is cleansed of all images,
it will contain them all.
Jalal al-Din Rumi (1207–73), Persia

GIVING

047. SIMPLE GIFTS

He who offers to me with devotion only a leaf, or a
flower, or a fruit, or even a little water, this I accept
from that yearning soul, because with a pure heart
it was offered with love.

From the *Bhagavad Gita* (1st–2nd century BCE), India

048. OTHERS

I am in love with all the gifts of the world, and
especially those destined for others to enjoy.

Santiago Bautista (1898–1937), Spain

049. THE GOOD THIEF

Others are my main concern.
When I notice something of mine,
I steal it and give it to others.
Shantideva (c.7th century), India

050. SHOWING THE WAY

Charity is incumbent on each person every day.
Charity is assisting anyone, moving and carrying
their wares, saying a good word. Every step one
takes walking to prayer is charity. Showing the way
is charity.
From the *Hadith* (c.7th century), the spoken Islamic
tradition attributed to the Prophet Muhammad

051. A NEED AND AN ECSTASY

For to the bee a flower is a fountain of life
And to the flower a bee is a messenger of love
And to both, bee and flower, the giving and the
   receiving of pleasure are a need and an ecstasy.
Kahlil Gibran (1883–1931), Lebanon/USA

052. GIVING IN POVERTY

One must be poor to know the luxury of giving.
George Eliot (1819–80), England

053. GOD'S WITNESS

You will not attain piety until you expend part
of what you love; and whatever you expend,
God knows of it.

From the *Koran*

054. ENERGIES OF GIVING

From the infinitely changeless vessel of spirit,
I savour the inexhaustible richness of generosity.

Eduardo Cuadra (1820-1903), Chile

THANKFULNESS

055. BREATHING

There are two graces in breathing: drawing in air and discharging it. The former constrains, the latter refreshes: so marvellously is life mixed. Thank God then when he presses you, and thank him again when he lets you go.

Johann Wolfgang von Goethe (1749–1832), Germany

056. THE COMPASS NEEDLE

As a needle turns to the north when it is touched by the magnet, so it is fitting O Lord, that I, your servant, should turn to love and praise and serve you – seeing that out of love for me you were willing to endure such grievous pangs and sufferings.

Ramon Llull (1232–1316), Spain

057. LOVE'S SWEETNESS

Jesus, how sweet is the very thought of you! The sweetness of your love surpasses the sweetness of honey. Nothing sweeter than you can be described. No words can express the joy of your love. Only those who have tasted your love for themselves comprehend it.

Thank you for giving yourself to us.

St Bernard of Clairvaux (1090–1153), France

058. THE SECRETARY

Of all the creatures both in sea and land,
Only to man thou hast made known thy ways,
And put the pen alone into his hand,
And made him secretary of thy praise.

George Herbert (1593–1633), from "Providence", England

WONDER

059. SOME THINGS...

Some things that fly there be
Birds – Hours – the Bumblebee –
Of these no Elegy.

Some things that stay there be –
Grief – Hills – Eternity –
Nor this behooveth me.

There are that resting, rise.
Can I expound the skies?
How still the Riddle lies!
Emily Dickinson (1830–86), USA

060. WONDERS EVERYWHERE

The purpose of miracles is to teach
us to see the miraculous everywhere.
St Augustine of Hippo (354–430), North Africa

061. THE WONDERS WITHIN

We carry within us the wonders we seek
without us.
Sir Thomas Browne (1605–82), England

062. THE CHORUS OF STARS

You set up the sky like a canopy and spread it out
like a tent. By a mere act of will you gave the Earth
stability when there was nothing to uphold it. You
established the firmament ... and set in order the
chorus of the stars to praise your magnificence.
Eucharistic Prayer (c.380), from the *Apostolic
Constitutions*, Syria

063. GOD'S GRANDEUR

The world is charged with the grandeur of God.
    It will flame out, like shining from shook foil;
    It gathers to a greatness, like the ooze of oil
Crushed. Why do men then now not reck his rod?
Generations have trod, have trod, have trod;
    And all is seared with trade; bleared, smeared with toil;
    And wears man's smudge and shares man's smell: the soil
Is bare now, nor can foot feel, being shod.

And for all this, nature is never spent;
    There lives the dearest freshness deep down things;
And though the last lights off the black West went
    Oh, morning, at the brown brink eastward, springs –
Because the Holy Ghost over the bent
    World broods with warm breast and with ah! bright wings.

Gerard Manley Hopkins (1844–89), England

064. BEING ALIVE

Everything is extraordinarily clear. I see the whole
landscape before me, I see my hands, my feet, my
toes, and I smell the rich river mud. I feel a sense of
tremendous strangeness and wonder at being alive.
Wonder of wonders.
The Buddha (c.563–c.483BCE), India

065. A STRING OF BEADS

There is a secret One inside us;
the planets in all the galaxies
pass through his hands like beads.
That is a string of beads one should
look at with luminous eyes.
Kabir (15th century), India

066. OPEN AND CLOSED EYES

The most beautiful thing we can experience
is the mysterious. ... He to whom this emotion
is a stranger – who can no longer pause to wonder
and stand rapt in awe – is as good as dead: his eyes
are closed.

Albert Einstein (1879–1955), Germany/USA

067. HIDDEN DEPTHS

Pascal wrote that "every religion which does not
affirm that God is hidden is not true". Mystery is the
oxygen of truth as well as the elixir of faith. Gross
certainties would undermine all our value.

Giuseppe Maraspini (1845–1910), Italy

068. A PHILOSOPHER'S ADMIRATION

Two things fill the mind with ever new and increasing admiration and awe, the oftener and more steadily we reflect on them: the starry heavens above and the moral law within.
Immanuel Kant (1724–1804), Germany

069. THE CALL OF NATURE

The call of moon and forest was irresistible. The storms of the monsoon season also called to me. ... When I hear it now, I pause ... and I listen with awe and passion.
Thich Nhat Hanh (b.1926), Vietnam

BEING IN TIME

070. PARADISE REGAINED

Mindfulness helps us to regain the paradise we thought we had lost ... If we sit firmly in the present moment, it is as though we are sitting on a lotus.
Thich Nhat Hanh (b.1926), Vietnam

071. THE INEXHAUSTIBLE MOMENT

The present moment is always full of infinite treasure. It contains far more than you can possibly grasp. Faith is the measure of its riches: what you find in the present moment is according to the measure of your faith. Love also is the measure: the more the heart loves, the more it rejoices in what God provides. The will of God presents itself at each moment like an immense ocean that the desire of your heart cannot empty; yet you will drink from that ocean according to your faith and love.
Jean-Pierre de Caussade (1675–1751), France

072. BE WHERE YOU ARE

As you walk and eat and travel, be where you are.
Otherwise you will miss most of your life.
The Buddha (c.563–c.483BCE), India

073. THE DRIED-UP RIVER

The riverbed, dried-up, half-full of leaves.
Us, listening to a river in the trees.
Seamus Heaney (1939–2013), epigraph to *The Haw
Lantern*, Ireland

074. THE TRUE DIMENSION

Let us not look back in anger or forward in fear,
but around in awareness.
James Thurber (1894–1961), USA

075. THE INSPIRATION OF BEING

Every blade of grass has its angel that bends over it and whispers, "Grow, grow."
From the *Talmud* (6th century)

076. STARTING NOW

How wonderful it is that nobody need wait a single moment before beginning to improve the world.
Anne Frank (1929–45), Netherlands

077. YESTERDAY AND TOMORROW

Try to strike that delicate balance
between a yesterday that should
be remembered
and a tomorrow that must be created.
Earl A Grollman (b.1925), USA

078. HOPING AND SLEEPING

Put off until tomorrow those tears which fill
    your eyes and your head,
Flooding you, rolling down your cheeks, those
    tears which stream down your cheek,
Because between now and tomorrow, maybe
    I, God, will have passed your way.
Human wisdom says: Woe to the man who
    puts off what he has to do until tomorrow.
And I say: Blessed, blessed is the man who
    puts off what he has to do until tomorrow.
Blessed is he who puts off –
That is to say, Blessed is he who hopes.
    And who sleeps.
Charles Péguy (1873–1914), France

079. BUTTERFLIES AND SUNLIGHT

I stood in a room that contained every moment –
a butterfly museum.

And the sun still as strong as before.
Its impatient brushes were painting the world.
Tomas Tranströmer (1931–2015), from "Secrets on
the Way", Sweden

080. THE PEBBLE

Should I now wish to examine a particular type of
stone more closely, I would choose the pebble,
both because of the perfection of its form and
because I can pick it up and turn it about in my
hand. Also the pebble is stone at the exact age
when personality, individuality – in other words
language – emerges. As compared to the rockbed
from which it derives directly, it is stone already
fragmented and polished into a great many almost
identical individuals. ...
While it lies there a few days longer, with no
practical significance, let us make the most of its
virtues.
Francis Ponge (1899–1988), France

081. PRAYER FROM THE MIDST OF THE SENSES

I was utterly alone with the sun and the earth. Lying down on the grass, I spoke in my soul to the earth, the sun, the air, and the distant sea far beyond sight.

I thought of the earth's firmness – I felt it bear me up; through the grassy couch there came an influence as if I could feel the great earth speaking to me.

I thought of the wandering air – its pureness, which is its beauty; the air touched me and gave me something of itself.

I spoke to the sea: though very far, in my mind I saw it, green at the rim of the earth and blue in deeper ocean.

I turned to the blue heaven again, gazing into its depth, inhaling its exquisite colour and sweetness. The rich blue of the unattainable flower of the sky drew my soul towards it, and there it rested, for pure colour is rest of heart.

By all these I prayed.

Then, returning, I prayed by the sweet thyme, whose little flowers I touched with my hand; by the slender grass; by the crumble of dry chalky earth I took up and let fall through my fingers. Touching the crumble of earth, the blade of grass, the thyme flower, breathing the earth-encircling air, thinking of the sea and the sky, holding out my hand for the sunbeams to touch it, prone on the sward in token of deep reverence, thus I prayed.

Richard Jefferies (1848–87), England

082. THE NARROW GATE

Every second of time is the narrow gate
through which enlightenment might enter.
Modern inspiration from Beijing

083. REFUGE

I take refuge with the Lord of the Daybreak.
From the *Koran*

084. TIME AND OURSELVES

We think in eternity, but we move slowly
through time.
Oscar Wilde (1854–1900), Ireland

085. THE SHARPNESS OF NOW

The moment is what you are in. Like a sword the moment cuts away everything around itself so that it can be free.
The sword is gentle to the touch and its edge is sharp.
Those who handle it gently are unharmed. But those who treat it roughly are injured.
Qushayri (c.986–1072), from the *Risalah*, Persia

086. INITIATION SONG

I have planted a footprint, a sacred one.
I have planted a footprint, through it the grass-blades push upward.
I have planted a footprint, through it the grass-blades radiate.
I have planted a footprint, over it the grass-blades float in the wind.
I have planted a footprint, over it I bend the stalk to pluck the ears.
I have planted a footprint, over it the blossoms lie gray.
I have planted a footprint, smoke arises from my house.
I have planted a footprint, I live in the light of day.
Anonymous (c.1900), USA

ATTENTIVENESS

087. THE RAIN STICK

Up-end the rain stick and what happens next
Is a music that you never would have known
To listen for. ...

Up-end the stick again. What happens next

Is undiminished for having happened once,
Twice, ten, a thousand times before.
Who cares if all the music that transpires

Is the fall of grit or dry seeds through a cactus?
You are like a rich man entering heaven
Through the ear of a raindrop. Listen now again.
Seamus Heaney (1939–2013), from "The Rain Stick",
Ireland

088. LOOKING

Thinking is more interesting than knowing, but less interesting than looking.

Johann Wolfgang von Goethe (1749–1832), Germany

089. BEYOND THE SENSES

Our eyes believe themselves, our ears believe other people, our intuition believes the truth of the spirit.

Adapted from a German proverb

NATURE

090. LOVE LETTERS

Everyday, priests minutely examine the Dharma and endlessly chant complicated *sutras*. Before doing that, though, they should learn how to read the love letters sent by the wind and rain, the snow and moon.

Ikkyú (1394–1481), Japan

091. MOON AND SUN

Our cup is the full moon; our wine is the sun.

Ibn al-Farid (1181–1235), Egypt

092. PREFERRED CHOICE

If one way be better than another, that, you may be sure, is nature's way.

Aristotle (384–322BCE), Greece

ACCEPTANCE

093. HEAVEN'S APPOINTMENTS

The superior person is quiet and calm, waiting patiently for Heaven's appointments. The inferior person treads a dangerous way, always on the look-out for good fortune.

Confucius (551–479BCE), China

094. THE EDUCATED WISH

Learn to wish that everything should come to pass exactly as it does.

Epictetus (c.55–c.135), Greece

095. THE UNIVERSE UNFOLDING

You are a child of the Universe, no less than the moon and the stars; you have a right to be here. And whether or not it is clear to you, no doubt the Universe is unfolding as it should.

Max Ehrmann (1872–1945), USA

096. LOVE AND JUDGMENT

Abba Xanthias said: A dog is better than I because it also has love, but it does not pass judgment.

From the sayings of the Desert Fathers (5th century), Egypt

097. THE COUNSEL OF PERFECTION

Do not seek perfection in a changing world. Instead, perfect your love.

Master Sengstan (c.496–606), China

098. WIND TO WILLOW

Willow, I have a desire to knock you over.
You bend so gracefully, so contentedly.

Grace is a wheatfield, grown from the seeds
of acceptance.
Anna Korolev (b.1960), Ukraine

099. HOLD ON, LET GO

One wears his mind out in study, and yet has more mind with which to study. One gives away his heart in love and yet has more heart to give away. One perishes out of pity for a suffering world, and is stronger therefore. So, too, it is possible at one and the same time to hold on to life and let go.

Milton Steinberg (1903–50), USA

100. WEATHER WISE

The gentle rain which waters my beans and keeps me in the house today is not drear and melancholy, but good for me too. Though it prevents my hoeing them, it is of far more worth than my hoeing. If it should continue so long as to cause the seeds to rot in the ground and destroy the potatoes in the low lands, it would still be good for the grass on the uplands, and, being good for the grass, it would be good for me.

Henry David Thoreau (1817–62), USA

SIMPLICITY

101. THE EGO AND THE SELF

Like two golden birds perched on a tree, the ego
and the self are united companions: one eats the
sweet and sour fruits of the tree, while the other
looks on without eating. As long as you identify
with the ego, you will feel attached to both joy and
sorrow. But if you know that you are the self, the
lord of life, you will be freed from suffering. You will
transcend duality and move into a state of Oneness.
From the *Bhagavad Gita* (1st–2nd century BCE), India

102. BE LIKE THE TORTOISE

When one withdraws all desires as a tortoise
withdraws its limbs, then the natural splendour
of the world soon manifests itself.
From the *Mahabharata* (c.400BCE–c.200CE), India

103. A POT AND ITS PURPOSE

The usefulness of a pot comes from its emptiness.
Lao Tzu (c.604–c.531BCE), from the *Tao Te Ching*,
China

104. ENOUGH

I think that maybe
I will be a little surer
of being a little nearer.
That is all. Eternity
is in the understanding
that little is more than enough.
R S Thomas (1913–2000), Wales

105. ETERNITY

He who binds to himself a joy
Does the winged life destroy;
But he who kisses the joy as it flies
Lives in eternity's sun rise.
William Blake (1757–1827), England

106. THREE QUESTIONS

In the end these things matter most: How well
did you love? How fully did you love? How deeply
did you learn to let go?
The Buddha (c.563–c.483BCE), India

HAPPINESS

107. THE REST OF JOY

The Holy Spirit does not rest where there is idleness,
or sadness, or ribaldry, or frivolity, or empty speech.
But only where there is joy.

From the *Midrash Psalms* (c.2nd century)

108. SOURCE OF CONTENTMENT

Beauty remains even in misfortune. If you just look
for it, you discover more and more happiness and
regain your balance. A person who's happy will
make others happy; a person who has courage
will never die in misery.

Anne Frank (1929–45), Netherlands

109. MOTHER'S SONG

it's quiet in the house so quiet
outside the snowstorm wails
the dogs curl up noses under their tails
my little son sleeps on his back
his mouth open
his belly rises and falls
breathing
is it strange if I cry for joy?
Anonymous (19th century), translated from the Inuit

110. TRUE CONTENTMENT

Happiness is found on the familiar highways of life;
contentment is a herb that grows very close to
the earth.
Melville Harcourt (20th century), USA

111. THE DOOR

The door of happiness does not open away from us: we cannot rush at it to push it open. It opens toward us and, therefore, nothing is required of us.
Søren Kierkegaard (1813–55), Denmark

112. YOU AND YOUR SHADOW

Speak or act with a pure mind, and happiness will follow you as your shadow, unshakable.
The Buddha (c.563–c.483BCE), India

TRUTH

113. THE LAW OF TRUTH AND LOVE

Those who know the truth are not equal to those
who love the truth.
Confucius (551–479BCE), China

114. THE GAZE TOWARD TRUTH

Those who love truth more than life itself turn away
from the fleeting things of time with all their souls.
To use an expression of Plato – God himself sets their
faces in the right direction.
Simone Weil (1909–43), France

115. THE SELF IN TRUTH'S EMBRACE

If you would swim on the bosom of the ocean of Truth, you must reduce yourself to a zero.

Mahatma Gandhi (1869–1948), India

116. REASON IN ITS PLACE

Lord, help me never to use my reason against the Truth.

Jewish prayer

117. EACH OF US
Truth exists only for each individual when
he produces it through his actions.
Søren Kierkegaard (1813–55), Denmark

118. LIVE THE TRUTH
Not everyone can see the truth, but everyone can
be the truth.
Franz Kafka (1883–1924), Austria

WORDLESSNESS

119. THE SCENT OF THE ROSE

Rose, we are your coronation. To the ancients
you were a pale cup with a simple rim.
Now to us you are the infinite concordance
of spirit unfolding – *Rosa seriatim*.

In your opulence you seem to be wearing gown
upon gown on a body of nothing but light –
yet each petal separately appears to disown
and dissolve all dress in its endless midnight.

Your fragrance has whispered name after name
to us across the void for centuries.
Again, suddenly, it hangs in the air like fame,

yet still the words escape us. Perhaps we've guessed
...
but all we live for is to open our memories
to that sweetness, and the hours it laid to rest.
after Rainer Maria Rilke (1875–1926), Austria
(*seriatim*: in a series, one after the other)

120. THE RULE OF MOONLIGHT

Close the language-door,
and open the love-window.

The moon won't use the door,
only the window.
Jalal al-Din Rumi (1207–73), Persia

121. AN AWAKENING

The word is fast asleep under the blanket
of the adjective. Shall I wake it up?
Labhshankar Thackar (1935–2016), India

122. BEFORE YOU SPEAK ...

Before you speak, ask yourself: is it kind, is it
necessary, is it true, does it improve on the silence?
Shirdi Sai Baba (1838–1918), India

123. EARTH

It's wonderful to think
Of such a long river
With no words in it.
Jay Ramsay (b.1946), England

HUMILITY

124. FLYING TOWARD THE SUN

Lord Jesus, I am not an eagle. All I have are the eyes
and the heart of one. In spite of my littleness, I dare
to gaze at the sun of love, and I long to fly toward it.
St Thérèse of Lisieux (1873–97), France

125. SOUL HOUSE

I am not worthy, Master and Lord, that you should
come beneath the roof of my soul; yet since in
your love toward all, you wish to dwell in me, in
boldness I come. You command, open the gates,
which you alone have made. And you will come
in, and enlighten my darkened reasoning. I believe
that you will do this, for you did not send away that
harlot who came to you with tears, nor cast out the
repenting tax-collector, nor reject the thief who
acknowledged your kingdom. But you counted
all of these as members of your band of friends.
You are blessed evermore.
St John Chrysostom (c.347–c.407), Turkey

126. AN OLD MAN'S ADVICE

A brother asked an old man: "What is humility?" And the old man said: "To do good to those who hurt you." The brother said: "If you cannot go that far, what should you do?" The old man replied: "Get away from them and keep your mouth shut."

From the sayings of the Desert Fathers (5th century), Egypt

127. BY CONTRAST

Humility like darkness reveals the heavenly lights.

Henry David Thoreau (1817–62), USA

128. SELF-ASSESSMENT

The Sage knows himself, but does not show himself.
He loves himself but does not value himself.
Lao Tzu (c.604–c.531BCE), from the *Tao Te Ching*,
China

129. FIT TO BE A PILGRIM

Would you be a pilgrim on the road to Love?
The first condition is that you make yourself
as humble as dust and ashes.
Ansari of Herat (1006–89), Afganistan

FAITH

130. NIGHT WALK

If a man wishes to be sure of the road he treads
on, he must close his eyes and walk in the dark.
St John of the Cross (1542–91), Spain

131. IMMUNITY

Belief is better than anything else, and it is best
when rapt – above paying its respects to anybody's
doubt whatsoever.
Robert Frost (1874–1963), USA

132. THE FLIGHT OF BEAUTY

Ah –
I patiently close my eyes on all the grins and smirks,
on all the twisted smiles and horse laughs –
and glimpse then, inside me,
one beautiful white butterfly
fluttering toward tomorrow.
Kuroda Saburo (1919–80), from "I Am Completely
Different", Japan

133. EL HOMBRE

It's a strange courage
you give me ancient star:

Shine alone in the sunrise
toward which you lend no part!
William Carlos Williams (1883–1963), USA

134. NIGHT AS DAY

If I take the wings of the morning and settle at
        the farthest limits of the sea,
even there your hand shall lead me, and your
        right hand shall hold me fast.
If I say, "Surely the darkness shall cover me,
        and the light around me become night,"
even the darkness is not dark to you; the night
        is as bright as the day, for darkness is as
        light to you.
Psalm 139:9–12

135. WINDOWS

He to whom worshipping is a window,
        to open but also to shut, has not
yet visited the house of his soul whose
        windows are open from dawn to dawn.
Kahlil Gibran (1883–1931), Lebanon/USA

136. 136 WONDERS UNSEEN

Keep your faith in beautiful things; in the sun
when it is hidden, in the Spring when it is gone.
Roy R Gibson (20th century), USA

137. THE THIRSTY FISH

I laugh when I hear that the fish in the water is thirsty.
I laugh when I hear that men go on pilgrimage to find
God.
Kabir (15th century), India

138. THE GREAT BEYOND

Faith begins where imagination ends.

Søren Kierkegaard (1813–55), Denmark

139. GOD'S CHILDREN

Beloved, we are God's children now; what we will be has not yet been revealed. What we do know is this: when he is revealed, we will be like him, for we will see him as he is.

1 John 3:2

140. THE FOUNTAIN OF LIFE

How precious is your steadfast love, O God!
    All people may take refuge in the shadow of your
wings.
They feast on the abundance of your house,
    and you give them drink from the river of your
delights.
For with you is the fountain of life;
    in your light we see light.

Psalm 36:7-9

141. A FOUNTAIN OF LEAVES

Deliver us from the long drought of the mind;
Let leaves from the deciduous cross fall on us
Washing us clean
Turning our autumn to gold
By the affluence of their fountain.

R S Thomas (1913-2000), Wales

142. SHINING FAITH

No coward soul is mine,

No trembler in the world's storm-troubled sphere.

I see Heaven's glories shine,

And Faith shines equal, arming me from Fear.

Emily Brontë (1818–48), from "No Coward Soul is Mine", England

143. EVERYWHERE THE DIVINE

God to surround me, God to encompass me;

God in my words, God in my thoughts;

God in my waking, God in my resting;

God in my hoping, God in my doing;

God in my heart, God in my soul;

God in my weakness, God in my strength;

God in my life, God in my eternity;

God in my life, God in my eternity.

W Mary Calvert (20th century), USA

The Inner Circle of Love

EMPATHY
144...148

SELFLESSNESS
149...154

COMPASSION
155...166

FRIENDSHIP
167...177

FAMILY
178...186

KARMA
187...194

EVERYDAY LOVE
195...209

SACRED UNION
210...215

MYSTIC LOVE
216...227

PARTINGS
228...230

NEW LIFE
231...240

EMPATHY

144. LOVING ALL

Never put anyone out of your heart ...
Maharaj-ji (c.1890–1973), India

145. ANOTHER'S SOUL

What have we seen of another person, when the shutters of the soul are closed? About as much as the cover of a book.
Sten Stensen Blicher (1782–1848), Denmark

146. THE SECRET HISTORY

If we could read the secret history of our enemies we should find in each man's life sorrow and suffering enough to disarm all hostility.

Henry Wadsworth Longfellow (1807–82), USA

147. COMPARISONS

Use all your faculties to appreciate God's love. Use your soul to understand other souls. Use your body to sympathize with other people's bodily experiences. Use your emotions of anger and revenge to understand war. Appreciate goodness by distinguishing it from evil. Enjoy every moment of life by constantly reminding yourself of the imminence of death.

St Hildegard von Bingen (1098–1179), Germany

148. HEALING WOUNDS

Our hearts are healthy in a sick way when we are not wounded by God's love. ... But they are wounded to be healed when God strikes insensible minds with the barbs of his love and soon renders them sensitive through the fire of charity.

St Gregory the Great (c.540–604), Rome

SELFLESSNESS

149. OTHERS' HAPPINESS

All happiness comes from the desire for others to be
happy.
All misery comes from the desire for oneself to be
happy.
Shantideva (c.685–763), India

150. HOW TO BE BROTHERS

None of you is a true believer until you wish for your
brother what you wish for yourself.
From the *Hadith* (c.7th century), the spoken Islamic
tradition attributed to the Prophet Muhammad

151. THE STORY OF THE SANDALS

One day Rabbi Tarfan's mother's sandals split and
broke, and as she could not mend them, she had to
walk across the courtyard barefoot. So Rabbi Tarfan
kept stretching his hands under her feet, so that she
might walk over them, all the way.
From the *Talmud* (6th century)

152. TRUE GIVING

The only gift is a portion of thyself.

Ralph Waldo Emerson (1803–82), USA

153. TRANSCENDENCE

To be selfless is to be all-pervading.
To be all-pervading is to be transcendent.

Lao Tzu (c.604–c.531BCE), from the *Tao Te Ching*,
China

154. THE SELF IN ITS PLACE

I will cease to live as a self and will take as my self
my fellow-creatures.

Shantideva (c.7th century), India

COMPASSION

155. THE TRANCE OF COMPASSION

By practicing kindness all over with everyone you will soon come into the holy trance, definite distinctions of personalities will become what they really mysteriously are, our common and eternal bliss-stuff, the pureness of everything forever, the great bright essence of mind, even and one thing everywhere the holy eternal milky love, the white light everywhere everything, empty-bliss, svaha, shining, ready, and awake, the compassion in the sound of silence, the swarming myriad trillionaire you are.

Jack Kerouac (1922–69), USA

156. THE MUSIC OF BEING

We can be spacious yet full of loving kindness; full of compassion, yet serene. Live like the strings of a fine instrument – not too taut but not too loose.

The Buddha (c.563–c.483BCE), India

157. A PROMISE

They whose minds are filled with kindness
will never enter a world dark with woes.
Tiruvalluvar (c.1st century BCE), India

158. A DUTY

The first duty of love is to listen.
Paul Tillich (1886–1965), USA

159. A WARNING

Listen, or your tongue will keep you deaf.
Native North American proverb

160. THE CHAIN OF LOVE

You shall not enter Paradise until you have faith, and
you cannot have faith until you love one another.
Have compassion on those you can see, and He
whom you cannot see will have compassion on you.
From the *Hadith* (c.7th century), the spoken Islamic
tradition attributed to the Prophet Muhammad

161. A NOBLE SOUL

A superior being does not render evil for evil.
Never harm the wicked or the good or even
criminals meriting death. A noble soul is always
compassionate, even toward those who enjoy
injuring others or who are actually committing
cruel deeds – for who is without fault?
From the *Ramayana* (c.300BCE), India

162. STRENGTH OF FEELING

True compassion flows fast, as if we were wounded
ourselves, yet without diminishing our strength.
Modern inspiration from Tokyo

163. PARENTS

It is the way of a father to be compassionate and it is
the way of a mother to comfort. The Holy One said:
"I will act like a father and a mother."
***Pesikta de-Rav Kahana* 19:3** (c.2nd century), India

164. DIMENSIONS

"And behold a wall on the outside of the house round about, and in the man's hand a measuring reed of six cubits long by the cubit and a hand breadth: so he measured the breadth of the building, one reed; and the height, one reed."
Ezekiel 40:5

Breadth pertains to charity for the neighbour; height to the understanding of the Maker. The breadth and the height of the building are measured at one cubit because each soul will be as high in knowledge of God as it is broad in love of neighbour. While it enlarges itself in width through love, it lifts itself in height through knowledge, and it is as high above itself as it extends outside itself in love of neighbour.
St Gregory the Great (c.540–604), Rome

165. THE SICK ROOM

I turn with love my face to your sickness.
If one atom of my heart shows a squeamish impulse
to run away,
  let it be said I am less whole than you.
I turn with love my face and loving touch
  to ease your sickness and give thanks for your
courage.
Let my closeness be my prayer for your renewal.
Maria Glauber (b.1953), Germany

166. ENDS, NOT MEANS

Act in such a way that you always treat humanity,
whether in your own person or in the person of any
other, never simply as a means, but always at the
same time as an end.
Immanuel Kant (1724–1804), Germany

FRIENDSHIP

167. THE HEART'S MORNING

And in the sweetness of friendship let there
be laughter, and sharing of pleasure,
For in the dew of little things the heart finds
its morning and is refreshed.
Kahlil Gibran (1883–1931), Lebanon/USA

168. STRONG AND SILENT

Our friendships are our secret resource,
our reinforcements.

No enemy quite knows their strength.

No true friends will count our enemies
before throwing themselves into the fray.

The love in friendship is never weaker
for being undeclared.

Some such loves remain silent forever,
like the moon.

The touch of a friend can feel like God's touch –
scarcely noticeable.
Anna Szczuka (b.1945), Poland

169. MATURING

A new friend is new wine; When it grows old,
you will enjoy drinking it.
Ben Sira (c.2nd century BCE), Israel

170. MIRROR AND WINDOW

Friend, be my mirror,
>tell me when I do wrong, or if you are too kind,
>let my failings show up in the frame of all your
virtues.

Friend, be my window,
>convince me that I live in a small cell of habit.
>I long to join you on the endless frontier of your
openness.
Lourdes Mallo (20th century), Gran Canaria

171. GOLD

How will you know your real friends?
Pain is as dear to them as life.
A friend is like gold. Trouble is like fire.
Pure gold delights in the fire.
Jalal al-Din Rumi (1207–73), Persia

172. ENRICHMENT

Always seek out friends who are wise, and perhaps
a little on the rigorous side – such company will be
spiritually enriching.
Otto Rix (1820–1903), Austria

173. THE SHELL OF FRIENDSHIP

The reflection cast from good friends is needed
  until you become with the aid of any reflector,
  a drawer of water from the Sea.
Know that the reflection is at first just imitation,
  but when it continues to recur,
  it turns into direct realization of truth.
Until it has become realization,
don't part from the friends who guide you –
  don't break away from the shell
if the raindrop hasn't yet become a pearl.
Jalal al-Din Rumi (1207–73), Persia

174. SILENT COMPANIONSHIP

If friendship is firmly established between two
hearts, they do not need to exchange news.
Sa'ib of Tabriz (c.1601–77), Persia

175. THE RULE OF THREE

Friendship with the virtuous, friendship with the sincere, friendship with the observant – these three friendships are advantageous.
Confucius (551–479BCE), China

176. SIGNIFICANT HOURS

I always think that we live, spiritually, by what others have given us in the significant hours of our life. These significant hours do not announce themselves as coming, but arrive unexpected.
Albert Schweitzer (1875–1965), France

177. ALL BUT A BIRD

Friendship is Love without his wing.
Lord Byron (1788–1824), England

FAMILY

178. "THE LOT OF LOVE IS CHOSEN"
W B Yeats

But do you choose, or else does love choose you?
Our common speech, that utters mysteries
Only half known, insists we *fall* in love.
Who voyages on those seas
Goes to the ends of the world, a lifetime's journey.
Yet vows are chosen, and acts that make them good
Chosen, for better, for worse, or hard or easy.

I search for words to bless you, find none right,
But see that you from stores of joy already
Are blessing others, while your joys increase.
Blest be your chosen lot, dear son and daughter,
And the journey you began before you willed it –
Falling in love – upon those passionate seas.
Anne Ridler (1912–2001), England

179. GROWING UP

When I asked you as a child
How high should fences be
To keep in the butterflies,
Blood was already passing
Down median and margin
To the apex of a wing.

Michael Longley (b.1939), from
"The White Butterfly", Northern Ireland

180. ANOTHER WAY

Don't limit a child to your own way of loving,
for he was born in another time.

Adapted from a Rabbinical saying

181. THE GIFT OF CIVILIZATION

I must study politics and war, that my sons may have
the liberty to study mathematics and philosophy,
geography, natural history, and naval architecture,
navigation, commerce, and agriculture, in order to
give their children a right to study painting, poetry,
music, architecture, statuary, tapestry and porcelain.
John Quincy Adams (1767–1848), USA

182. A WISH FOR MY CHILDREN

On this doorstep I stand
year after year
and watch you leaving

and think: May you not
skin your knees. May you
not catch your fingers
in car doors. May
your hearts not break.

May tide and weather
wait for your coming

and may you grow strong
to break
all webs of my weaving.
Evangeline Paterson (1928–2000), England

183. THE LORD'S BLESSING

Behold, children are a
blessing from the Lord.
The fruit of the womb is a reward.
Like the arrows in the hand of a warrior,
so are the children of one's youth.
Happy is the man who
has his quiver full of them.

Psalm 127:3–5

 184. THE FLAG OF LOVE

Our son and daughter treasure the tattered flag of
our love.
This banner survived their revolution.
Threadbare now, it has become unutterably
precious.
Like embers, it glows with familial warmth whenever
their
breath comes close enough.
We know that one day its threads and colors will be
bathed
in the renewing spring of a grandchild's cry for
freedom.

Esther Cohen (b.1971), USA

185. QUESTION AND ANSWER

What is the best thing I can do for you, my children?
Love yourself and love our mother.
Joann Hertzberger (1899–1960), Netherlands

186. FOREVER YOUNG

Youth never disappears, for it is still in harmony with the Divine.
Alexandre Dumas (1802–70), France

KARMA

187. THE RULE OF RETURNS

Whoever gives reverence receives reverence: whoever brings sugar eats almond cake.

Jalal al-Din Rumi (1207–73), Persia

188. OBLIGATION

We have no more right to consume happiness without producing it than to consume wealth without producing it.

George Bernard Shaw (1856–1950), Ireland

189. ON TWO WHEELS

The success of one's actions rests equally on destiny
and on personal effort. Destiny is the fruit of efforts
made in a previous life. As a chariot cannot move on
one wheel alone, so without personal effort destiny
alone accomplishes nothing.
Yajnavalkya smriti 1:349–53, India

190. NOURISHMENT

The reward for a good deed performed in this world
will be enjoyed in the next world; when one waters
the roots of trees, fruits form at their branches.
Subhashitarnava 271, India

191. LIFESAVERS

Whoever saves one life, it is as if he saved the
entire world.
From the *Talmud* (6th century)

192. THE SWORD

Then Jesus said to him, "Put your sword back into
its place; for all those who take the sword will perish
by the sword..."
Matthew 26:52

193. YOUR SHADOW

Rise up to the heavens or move to the ends of the world, plunge into the deep sea or stay where you are: the consequences of works that bring fortune and misfortune to people, accumulated in previous lives, will follow you like a shadow.

Sahityadarpana 3:21 (c.14th century), India

194. LIGHT AND DARK

There are two ways of passing from this world – one in light and one in darkness. Someone who passes in light does not come back; but someone who passes in darkness returns.

From the *Bhagavad Gita* (1st–2nd century BCE), India

EVERYDAY LOVE

195. LOVE IN DAILY USE

And here is love
like a tinsmith's scoop
sunk past its gleam
in the meal-bin.
Seamus Heaney (1939–2013), from "Mossbawn:
Two Poems in Dedication", Ireland

196. WORK AND WIND

My fine strong horse
can pull a heavy plough
and never tire.

Yet it can also gallop
through a wild country.

I am working hard at love,
with the wind in my hair.
José Morazán (b.1952), Honduras

197. BY DAY AND NIGHT

Togetherness: to pray together by day in blessed harness, and rest together by night in mystic peace.
Juliana Pereira (1895–1976), Portugal

198. REVELATIONS

There is nothing that will not reveal its secrets if you love it enough.
George Washington Carver (1864–1943), USA

199. A SHELTER FOR SOLITUDE

I hold this to be the highest task for a
bond between two people, that each protects the
solitude of the other.

Rainer Maria Rilke (1875–1926), Austria

200. RESISTANCE

Let us love the country of here below.
It is real; it offers resistance to love.

Simone Weil (1909–43), France

201. HARMONY

Stand off from me; be still your own;
Love's perfect chord maintains the sense
Through harmony, not unison,
Of finest difference.
Edward Dowden (1843–1913), from
"Love's Chord", Ireland

202. LETTING GO

We need in love to practise only this: letting each
other go. For holding on comes easily – we do not
need to learn it.
Rainer Maria Rilke (1875–1926), Austria

203. SIDE BY SIDE

Life has taught me that love does not consist
in gazing at each other but in looking outward
together in the same direction.
Antoine de Saint-Exupéry (1900–44), France

204. THE PHILOSOPHY OF LOVE

Good is the magnetic centre towards which love
naturally moves. False love moves to false good.
False love embraces false death. When true good
is loved, even impurely or by accident, the quality
of the love is automatically refined, and when the
soul is turned towards Good the highest part of the
soul is enlivened. Love is the tension between the
imperfect soul and the magnetic perfection which is
conceived of as lying beyond it. ... And when we try
perfectly to love what is imperfect our love goes to
its object *via* the Good to be thus purified and made
unselfish and just. ... Love is the general name of the
quality of attachment and it is capable of infinite
degradation and is the source of our greatest errors;
but when it is even partially refined it is the energy
and passion of the soul in its search for Good, the
force that joins us to Good and joins us to the world
through Good. Its existence is the unmistakable
sign that we are spiritual creatures, attracted by
excellence and made for the Good. It is a reflection
of the warmth and light of the sun.
Iris Murdoch (1919–99), England

205. WORKING WITH LOVE

And what is it to work with love?
It is to weave the cloth with threads drawn
    from your heart, even as if your beloved
    were to wear that cloth.
It is to build a house with affection, even as
    if your beloved were to dwell in that house.
It is to sow seeds with tenderness and reap
    the harvest with joy, even as if your
    beloved were to eat the fruit.
Kahlil Gibran (1833–1931), Lebanon/USA

206. BEYOND THE REFLECTION

The beginning of love is to let those we love be
perfectly themselves, and not to
twist them to fit our own image. Otherwise we love
only the reflection of ourselves we find in them.
Thomas Merton (1915–68), USA

207. A MOONLIT NIGHT

There is a way from your heart to mine
    and my heart knows it,
because it is clean and pure like water.
    When the water is still like a mirror,
    it can behold the Moon.
Jalal al-Din Rumi (1207–73), Persia

208. THE CHALLENGE

For one human being to love another: that is
perhaps the most difficult of all our tasks, the
ultimate, the last test and proof, the work for
which all other work is but preparation.
Rainer Maria Rilke (1875–1926), Austria

209. SEEING THINGS ANEW

I am the silk page at your fingertips
running down on me, the fruit you revolve
and leave mapped in bloom, the blur of a lens
you lift a shirt hem to, rub over, breathe on,
I am the way you see the world anew.

Mimi Khalvati (b.1944), from "Tenderness", England

SACRED UNION

210. WONDER IN MY HEART

... here is the deepest secret nobody knows
(here is the root of the root and the bud of the bud
and the sky of the sky of a tree called life; which
grows
higher than the soul can hope or mind can hide) and
this is the wonder that's keeping the stars apart

i carry your heart(i carry it in my heart)
e e cummings (1894–1962), from "i carry your heart
with me(i carry it in my heart)", USA

211. AS I DIG FOR WILD ORCHIDS

As I dig for wild orchids
in the autumn fields,
it is the deeply-bedded root
that I desire,
not the flower.
Izumi Shikibu (c.974–c.1034), Japan

212. BLESSING FOR A LOVER

You are the star of each night,
You are the brightness of every morning,
You are the story of each guest
You are the report of every land.

No evil shall befall you. On hill or bank,
In field or valley. On mountain or in glen.

Neither above nor below. Neither in sea
Nor on shore,
In skies above. Nor in the depths.

You are the kernel of my heart,
You are the face of my sun,
You are the harp of my music,
You are the crown of my company.
Modern Celtic blessing from Ireland

213. SOULMATES

Heart, are you great enough
    For a love that never tires?
O heart, are you great enough for love?
I have a heart of thorns and briers.
Over the thorns and briers,
    Over the meadows and stiles,
Over the world to the end of it
    Flash for a million miles.

Alfred, Lord Tennyson (1809–92), from "Marriage Morning", England

214. FOR A WEDDING

This is the chaste kiss of our union:
    for one miraculous moment
    all nature is our congregation and our choir.
We have the ear and eye of heaven.
The One smiles in our hearts.

No moment could be more sacred in our lives.
    We rejoice that we are thought worthy to be
    actors in the peaceful drama of blissful souls.
We have the hope and courage of heaven.
The One smiles in our hearts.
Manon Williams (1920–2001), Wales

215. TO MY DEAR AND LOVING HUSBAND

If ever two were one, then surely we.
If ever man were loved by wife, then thee.
If ever wife were happy in a man,
Compare with me, ye women, if you can.
I prize thy love more than whole mines of gold
Or all the riches that the East doth hold.
My love is such that rivers cannot quench
Nor ought but love from thee, give recompense.
Anne Bradstreet (c.1612–72), England/USA

MYSTIC LOVE

216. THE HALO

My soul gave me good counsel, teaching me to love. Love was for me a delicate thread stretched between two adjacent pegs, but now it has been transformed into a halo; its first is its last, and its last is its first. It encompasses every being, slowly expanding to embrace all that ever will be.
Jalal al-Din Rumi (1207–73), Persia

217. THE PEACE YOU BRING

And for what, except for you, do I feel love?
Do I press the extremest book of the wisest man
Close to me, hidden in me day and night?
In the uncertain light of single, certain truth,
Equal in living changingness to the light
In which I meet you, in which we sit at rest,
For a moment in the central of our being,
The vivid transparence that you bring is peace.
Wallace Stevens (1879–1955), prologue to
"Notes Toward a Supreme Fiction", USA

218. ETERNAL FIRE

But true love is a durable fire
In the mind ever burning;
Never sick, never old, never dead,
From itself never turning.

Walter Raleigh (c.1552–1618), from "As Ye Came
from the Holy Land of Walsinghame", England

219. KING SOLOMON'S WEDDING

King Solomon made himself a chariot of the wood of
Lebanon.

He made the pillars thereof of silver, the bottom
thereof of gold, the covering of it of purple, the
midst thereof being paved with love, for the
daughters of Jerusalem.

Go forth, O ye daughters of Zion, and behold King
Solomon with the crown wherewith his mother
crowned him in the day of his espousals, and in the
day of the gladness of his heart.

Song of Solomon 3:9–11

220. UNION

In so far as love is union, it knows no extremes
of distance.

Juana Inés de la Cruz (1651–95), Mexico

221. BEYOND THE MIND

Go to the truth beyond the mind. Love is the bridge.

Stephen Levine (1937–2016), USA

222. THE KISS OF PEACE

Love overflows into all:
From the glorious ocean's depths
    to beyond the farthest star,
Bounteous in loving all creation;
For to the King most High
Love has given her kiss of peace.

St Hildegard von Bingen (1098–1179), Germany

223. PERFECT VISION

If I glow on thee with the flame of love beyond all
that is seen on earth so that I overcome the power
of thine eyes, do not marvel, for it comes from
perfect vision, which, as it apprehends, moves
towards the apprehended good. I see well how
there shines now in thy mind the eternal light which,
seen, alone and always kindles love; and if aught else
beguile your love it is nothing but some trace of this,
ill-understood, that shines through thee.

Dante Alighieri (1265–1321), *Paradiso*, Canto V
(Beatrice addressing Dante), Italy

224. HIS MUSIC

I am in love and want the world to see.
I have carved the many names of God
      onto all the trees
within the sacred grove of my heart
      from which His music plays.

I am in love and want the world to hear.
I have no doubt His music will charm
      tiger and lion, snake and bullet ant,
disarm logger and poacher,
      bandit and tax collector.
From a folk song, Senegal

225. LOVE'S BEAUTY

Were I to promise love in a hundred thousand
languages, love's beauty far surpasses all such
stammerings.
Jalal al-Din Rumi (1207–73), Persia

226. TRANSFORMATIONS

Love turns a battery of stings into a paradise of honey. Love sets the slave on a golden throne.

Modern inspiration from Turkey

227. THE ASTROLABE OF GOD'S MYSTERIES

The lover's ailment is not like any other;
Love is the astrolabe of God's mysteries.
Whether Love is from heaven or earth,
    it points to God.

Jalal al-Din Rumi (1207–73), Persia

PARTINGS

228. LANDSCAPES

Watching the distant darkening hills, the trees
bending with the black weight of your absence,
I think of you ... and you are always with me,
watching the clouds hurry over the dangerous
waking seas, the islands biding their time like whales.
Let us smile together, safe in our love that conquers
distance, contented even in the bleak landscapes
of separation.

Paolo Marinetti (1799–1853), Italy

229. RESERVES OF SWEETNESS

Now we must draw, as plants would,
On tubers stored in a better season,
Our honey and heaven;
Only our love can store such food.
Anne Ridler (1912–2001), from "At Parting", England

230. WITH MY BLESSING

You're leaving me. Then go in peace. And let
Your wish alone be lamp to light your path,
And find tranquillity where'er you be.
Chaim Nachman Bialik (1873–1934), from
"You're Leaving Me", Israel

NEW LIFE

231. THE EVERYDAY MIRACLE

When people truly open their minds, and
contemplate the way in which the universe
is ordered and governed, they are amazed –
overwhelmed by a sense of the miraculous.
When people contemplate with open minds the
germination of a single seed, they are equally
overwhelmed – yet numerous babies are born every
day, and no-one marvels. If only people opened
their minds, they would see that the birth of a baby,
in which a new life is created, is a greater miracle
than restoring life.

St Augustine of Hippo (354–430), North Africa

232. CLOUDS OF GLORY

Our birth is but a sleep and a forgetting:
The soul that rises with us, our life's star,
    Hath had elsewhere its setting,
        And cometh from afar:
    Not in entire forgetfulness,
    And not in utter nakedness,
But trailing clouds of glory do we come
    From God, who is our home:
Heaven lies about us in our infancy!
William Wordsworth (1770–1850), from
"Ode: Intimations of Immortality", England

233. THE CATALYST

Long after the birth,
she held up the X-ray
of her second-born son
in the womb.

There he hung
against the light,
head-down to the lintel,
translucent
as wax in a glass.

What she saw
was not simply
the curve of the spine,
the seal at the cervix,

but sacrament brightly stilled;
an angelical stone
that cannot be weighed;

the catalyst
of sun through wax –
the ghostly body –
at the casual supper
Christ eating the honeycomb.
Pauline Stainer (b.1941), England

234. THE LIVING YES

As I am innocent, everything I do
Or say is couched in the affirmative.
Derek Mahon (b.1941), from "An Unborn Child",
Ireland

235. FOR A NEW-BORN CHILD

Blessing, sleep and grow taller in sleeping.
Lie ever in kind keeping.
Infants curl in a cowrie of peace
And should lie lazy. After this ease,
When the soul out of its safe shell goes,
Stretched as you stretch those knees and toes,
What should I wish you? Intelligence first,
In a credulous age by instruction cursed.
Take from us both what immunity
We have from the germ of the printed lie.
Your father's calm temper I wish you, and
The shaping power of his confident hand.
Much, too, that is different and your own;
And may we learn to leave you alone.
For your part, forgive us the pain of living,
Grow in that harsh sun great-hearted and loving.
Anne Ridler (1912–2001), from "For a Christening",
England

236. THE SEED

The greatest dreams on Earth
I trust to you my child.
You are the seed of humankind,
the hope, the future of the world.
Trán Düc Uyén (20th century), from
"A Letter to My Future Child", Vietnam

237. GREETING THE WORLD

Long time before
I in my mother's womb was born,
A God preparing did this glorious store,
The world, for me adorn.
Into this Eden so divine and fair,
So wide and bright, I come His son and heir.

A stranger here
Strange things doth meet, strange glories see;
Strange treasures lodged in this fair world appear,
Strange all, and new to me.
But that they mine should be, who nothing was,
That strangest is of all, yet brought to pass.
Thomas Traherne (1637–74), from "The Salutation",
England

238. A DIFFICULT JOY

For birth is awaking, birth is effort and pain;
And now at midwinter are the hints, inklings
(Sodden primrose, honeysuckle greening)
That sleep must be broken.
To bear new life or learn to live is an exacting joy:
The whole self must waken; you cannot predict the way
It will happen, or master the responses beforehand.
Anne Ridler (1912–2001), from "Christmas and Common Birth", England

239. FULLY ALIVE

I will not die an unlived life.
I will not live in fear
of falling or catching fire.
I choose to inhabit my days,
to allow my living to open me,
to make me less afraid,
more accessible,
to loosen my heart until it becomes a wing,
a torch, a promise.
I choose to risk my significance;
to live so that which came to me as seed
goes to the next as blossom
and that which came to me as blossom,
goes on as fruit.
Dawna Markova (b.1942), USA

240. A CHILD ASLEEP IN ITS OWN LIFE

Among the old men that you know,
There is one, unnamed, that broods
On all the rest, in heavy thought.

They are nothing, except in the universe
Of that single mind. He regards them
Outwardly and knows them inwardly,

The sole emperor of what they are,
Distant, yet close enough to wake
The chords above your bed to-night.
Wallace Stevens (1879–1955), USA

The Outer Circle of Spirit

IN TIMES OF DARKNESS
241...253

A WORLD OF PEACE
309...313

THE WAY
254...280

THE ONE
314...334

A WORLD OF KINSHIP
281...292

NEAR AND FAR HORIZONS
335...359

A WORLD OF HARMONY
293...308

ETERNITY
360...365

IN TIMES OF DARKNESS

241. THE AWAKENING

After the life and the dream
    comes what matters most:
        the awakening.
Don Paterson (b.1963), after Antonio Machado
(1875–1939), Spain

242. PATIENCE

Our real blessings often appear to us in the
shapes of pains, losses and disappointments;
but let us have patience, and we soon shall
see them in their proper figures.
Joseph Addison (1672–1719), England

243. THE DARK NIGHT OF THE SOUL

Even though the night darkens your spirit, its purpose is to impart light. Even though it humbles you, revealing the depth of your wretchedness, its purpose is to exalt and uplift you. Even though it empties you of all feeling and detaches you from all natural pleasures, its purpose is to fill you with spiritual joy and attach you to the source of that joy.

St John of the Cross (1542–91), Spain

244. FOOTPRINTS

You are the sweet kernel of adversity,
    the rescue that sets an ambush
    for all the world's kidnappers.
Your compassion dwells in the cave-
    city of all the world's desperados.
You are to be found within, above;
    but also I can see your footprints
    crisscrossing all the
    world's deserts.
Amicai Weizman (1888–1950), Israel

245. HOPE

Do not despair, saying, "My life is gone, and the
Friend has not come." He comes ... and out of season.
He comes not only at dawn.
Jalal al-Din Rumi (1207–73), Persia

246. BITTER-SWEET

Ah my dear angry Lord,
Since thou dost love, yet strike;
Cast down, yet help afford;
Sure I will do the like.

I will complain, yet praise;
I will bewail, approve:
And all my sour-sweet days
I will lament and love.
George Herbert (1593–1633), England

247. FRAGRANT LOVE

Wine sweetened with honey is used to pacify bees – When the bees smell this pungent and pleasant odour, they become peaceful; they sit quietly, relishing the fragrance. Similarly, when our hearts are in turmoil, God pours his spiritual wine into us – and all the warring powers of the soul fall into a delightful repose. We feel and sense nothing except the fragrance of God's love – we simply enjoy God.

Francis de Sales (1567–1622), France

248. THE LOVING GAZE

A Sufi master was sitting quietly, when a group of men came to punish him for wrongs he was accused of committing. The men rained blows on the Sufi master, hitting him a thousand times. Yet the Sufi master remained silent, and no sign of pain appeared on his face.

After they had finished beating him, the men took the Sufi master to the court.

The judges asked: "How did you suffer no pain when you were beaten?"

The Sufi master replied: "When the men were raining blows on me, my beloved wife was looking on. Her love made the pain seem easier. Then I thought that, if the loving gaze of a human being can ease pain, the loving gaze of God can eliminate pain altogether."

Nasir al-Din (1201–74), Persia

249. NATURE'S NOURISHMENT

No place of exile is so barren that
it can't abundantly support a man.
It's the mind that creates our wealth
and this goes with us into exile, and
in the harshest desert places it finds
enough to nourish the body and revels
in the enjoyment of its own goods.
Seneca (c.4BCE–c.65CE), Rome

250. HEART'S EASE

Cliffs that rise a thousand feet
    without a break,
Lakes that stretch a hundred miles
    without a wave,
Sands that are white through all the year,
    without a stain,
Pine-tree woods, winter and summer,
    ever green,
Streams that forever flow and flow
    without a pause,
Trees that for twenty thousand years
    your vows have kept,
You have suddenly healed the pain of a
    traveller's heart.
Chang Fang-sheng (4th century), China

251. THE SOLITARY TRAVELLER

Although they have tightly bound
    my arms and legs,
All over the mountains I hear the
    song of birds,
And the forest is filled
With the perfume of spring flowers.
Who can prevent me from freely
    enjoying these,
Which take from the long journey
A little of its loneliness?

Ho Chi Minh (1890–1969), from *Prison Diary*, Vietnam

252. TROUBLED SHORES

A great man does not lose his self-possession when he is afflicted; the ocean is not made muddy by the falling of its banks.

From the *Panchatantra* (6th century), India

253. ACCEPTANCE

If you are irritated by every rub,
how will your mirror be polished?

Jalal al-Din Rumi (1207–73), Persia

THE WAY

254. THE AMBITIOUS SOUL

The way is not inconsequential, whether we move forward or backward along it. The place and the way are inside a person. The place is the blissful state of the ambitious soul, the way is the constant change of the ambitious soul.

Søren Kierkegaard (1813–55), Denmark

255. THE RIDDLE OF THE PATH

You cannot tread the Path before you become the Path yourself.

Zen saying

256. ON SOLID GROUND

The old men used to say: If you see a young person climbing up to heaven by his own will, hold him by the foot, and pull him down to the ground, for it is just not good for him.

From the sayings of the Desert Fathers (5th century), Egypt

257. TRAVEL EASY

Easy is right.
Begin right and you are easy.
Continue easy and you are right.
Chuang Tzu (c.370–287BCE), China

258. A SOCRATIC PRAYER

Dear Pan and all other gods of this place, grant that I may become good in my heart. May my external possessions not be at war with what is within. Let me regard the wise man as rich. And let my store of gold be no more than a man of moderation can pick up and carry away.

Socrates (470–399BCE), Greece

259. ENERGY AND CALM

If you can work sincerely and correctly on what is at hand, and do so with energy and calm, not allowing distractions, but keeping your spirit pure, as if you had only borrowed it … hoping for nothing, fearing nothing, but satisfied with modulating your actions to the way of Nature, and with fearless truth in every word you utter, you will live contentedly. And no one can take that from you.

Marcus Aurelius (121–180), Rome

260. TO BE GREAT, BE WHOLE

To be great, be whole: do not exaggerate or
    exclude anything of what is yours.
Be entire in everything. Put all that you are
    into the least you do.
Be like the full moon, living aloft and
    shining everywhere.
Fernando Pessoa (1888–1935), Portugal

261. LOVE'S WINGS

The way to heaven is within. Shake the wings of love
– when love's wings have become strong, there is no
need to trouble about a ladder.
Jalal al-Din Rumi (1207–73), Persia

262. THE FOLLOWERS

To Him who is everywhere, folk come not by
travelling but by loving.
St Augustine of Hippo (354–430), North Africa

263. THE CALL

Come, my Way, my Truth, my Life:
Such a Way, as gives us breath:
Such a Truth, as ends all strife:
Such a Life, as killeth death.

Come, my Light, my Feast, my Strength:
Such a Light, as shows a feast:
Such a Feast, as mends in length:
Such a Strength, as makes his guest.

Come, my Joy, my Love, my Heart:
Such a Joy, as none can move:
Such a Love, as none can part:
Such a Heart, as joys in love.

George Herbert (1593–1633), England

264. LOOKING AND ASKING

Stand at the crossroads, and look,
  and ask for the ancient paths,
where the good way lies, and walk in it,
  and find rest for your souls.

Jeremiah 6:16

265. PATHS AND DESERTS

The earth beneath our feet takes many forms. Some only ride on paths, while others ride across trackless deserts. Those who ride on paths are like those who can see the way to God. Those who ride across trackless deserts are like those who have lost the way to God. Yet God reveals himself within the souls of both; he is the inner reality of all humankind.

Ibn al-'Arabi (1165–1240), Spain

266. CONTRADICTIONS

Only when you drink from the river of silence shall
    you indeed sing,
and when you have reached the mountain top, then
you
    shall begin to climb.
And when the earth shall claim your limbs, then shall
    you truly dance.

Kahlil Gibran (1883–1931), Lebanon/USA

267. STRIVING

By attempting the impossible one can attain the highest level of the possible.

August Strindberg (1849–1912), Sweden

268. HOW TO LIVE

Let the beauty we love be what we do.

Jalal al-Din Rumi (1207–73), Persia

269. STORIES

Maybe there are only three kinds of stories:
The stories we live,
The stories we tell,
And the stories that help our souls
Fly up towards the greater light.
Ben Okri (b.1959), Nigeria

270. THE WAY OF EXPERIENCE

Let me use suspense as material for perseverance:
Let me use danger as material for courage:
Let me use reproach as material for long suffering:
Let me use praise as material for humility:
Let me use pleasure as material for temperance:
Let me use pain as material for endurance.
John Baillie (1886–1960), Scotland

271. OUR LIFE

The fact that our task is exactly as large as our life makes it infinite.

Franz Kafka (1883–1924), Austria

272. THE MOTIVE FOR WORSHIP

O God! if I worship Thee in fear of Hell, burn me in Hell; and if I worship Thee in hope of Paradise, exclude me from Paradise; but if I worship Thee for Thine own sake, withold not Thine Everlasting Beauty!

Rabi'a al-Adawiyya (c.717–801), Mesopotamia

273. THE CLOUD OF UNKNOWING

Lift up your heart to God with humble love; and mean God himself, and not what you get out of him. When you first begin, you find only darkness, and as it were a cloud of unknowing – but still go on longing after him whom you love. For if you are to feel him or to see him in this life, it must always be in this cloud, in this darkness.

Julian of Norwich (c.1342–c.1416), England

274. FLOWERS OF THE SPIRIT

We may speak of love and humility as the true flowers of spiritual growth; and they give off a wonderful scent, which benefits all those who come near. The purpose of ecstatic prayer is to enable these flowers to bloom – In ecstatic prayer, without any effort, the Lord raises the soul from the Earth and lifts it to Heaven.

St Teresa of Avila (1515–82), Spain

275.  REMEMBRANCE

Remembrance of what is good keeps us high in spirit. Remembrance of what is beautiful is the salvation of mortal men. Remembrance of what is dear will be happiness, if it remains alive. Remembrance of the One is still the best thing I know.

Johann Wolfgang von Goethe (1749–1832), Germany

276. PETAL PATH

Once we have found the true path, our destiny unfolds itself like a long carpet of glorious flowers.

Jeanne Deneuve (20th century), France

277. IN READINESS

One should be ever booted and spurred and ready to depart.

Michel Eyquem de Montaigne (1533–92), France

278. OFFSHORE

We do not discover new lands without consenting to lose sight of the shore for a very long time.

André Gide (1869–1951), France

279. HOMECOMING

Home is not around the hearth,
    it is within the heart.
Any worthwhile pilgrimage brings us home,
    and so does any distant voyage
    for the sake of love.
Donald Masterson (20th century), from "Love's Compass", Canada

280. EXULTATION...

Exultation is the going
Of an inland soul to sea,
Past the houses – past the headlands –
Into deep Eternity –

Bred as we, among the mountains,
Can the sailor understand
The divine intoxication
Of the first league out from land?
Emily Dickinson (1830–86), USA

A WORLD OF KINSHIP

281. THE SONG OF DIFFERENCE

The more we let each voice sing
    out with its own true tone,
the richer will be the diversity of
    the chant in unison.
Angelus Silesius (1624–77), Poland

282. GENTLE STRENGTH

When spiders unite, they can tie up a lion.
Ethiopian proverb

283. THE ACQUISITION OF EXCELLENCE

Appreciation is a wonderful thing. It makes what is excellent in others belong to us as well.
Voltaire (1694–1778), France

284. A PERFECT CHORD

The diversity of the family should be a cause of love and harmony, as it is in music where many different notes blend together in the making of a perfect chord.

From the *Baha'i Scriptures* (19th century), Persia

285. HOSPITALITY

The runaway slave came to my house and stopped
    outside,
I heard his motions crackling the twigs of the
    woodpile,
Through the swung half-door of the kitchen I saw him
    limpsy and weak,
And went where he sat on a log and led him in and
    assured him,
And brought water and filled a tub for his sweated
    body and bruised feet,
And gave him a room that entered from my own, and I
    gave him some coarse clean clothes,
And remember perfectly well his revolving eyes and
    his awkwardness,
And remember putting plasters on the galls of his neck
    and ankles;
He stayed with me a week before he was recuperated
    and passed north.
I had him sit next me at table, my fire-lock leaned in
    the corner.

Walt Whitman (1819–92), from "Song of Myself", USA

286. ENTERTAINING STRANGERS

Let brotherly love continue.
Be not forgetful to entertain
strangers: for thereby some have
entertained angels unawares.
Hebrews 13:1

287. PRAYING AND LOVING

He prayeth well, who loveth well
Both man and bird and beast.
Samuel Taylor Coleridge (1772–1834), England

288. THE HEART'S NEW CAPITAL

Gentle souls, walk with me sometimes through
the breath of strangers, which parts like rain,
tremblingly brushes your cheeks, then behind
you with a parting tremble joins together again.

Strong, compassionate ones who reach the plateau
of the heart's new capital, settle here, mark
how your arrows love the bull's-eye and the bow,
how tears extend your eyesight through the dark.

Don't be afraid to suffer. Learn to give back
heaviness to the dead weight of the Earth,
its mountains and seas, nothingness to the black

hole inside the Earth's core. Though all the trees
you planted as children now have the girth
of monsters, still there are spaces ... and the breeze.
after Rainer Maria Rilke (1875–1926), Austria

289. MY CONGREGATION

Wherever I am, there in spirit is my congregation also – I cannot be separated from my people. We may be separated by space but we are united by love – even if my body dies, my soul will survive – and my soul will remember my people.

My congregation is my family; its members are my parents, my brothers and sisters, and my children. They are dearer to me than light – their love is weaving for me a crown that I shall wear for all eternity.

St John Chrysostom (c.347–c.407), Turkey

290. BELONGING

We owe our respect to a collectivity of whatever kind – country, family or any other – not for itself, but because it is food for a certain number of human souls.

Simone Weil (1909–43), France

291. ONE SOUL

I believe in the absolute oneness of God and therefore also of humanity. What though we have many bodies? We have but one soul.

Mahatma Gandhi (1869–1948), India

292. BREAD AND WATER

Our bread and water are of one table: the progeny of Adam are as a single soul.

Muhammad Iqbal (1877–1938), India

A WORLD OF HARMONY

293. LOVE THE WHOLE TREE

Love not the shapely branch,
Nor place its image alone in your heart.
It dies away.

Love the whole tree;
Then you will love the shapely branch,
The tender and withered leaf,
The shy bud and the full-blown flower,
The falling petal and the dancing night,
The splendid shadow of full love.

Ah, love Life in its fullness.
It knows no decay.
Jiddu Krishnamurti (1895–1986), India

294. THE HUMBLE WORM

Lands that are subject to frequent inundations are always poor; and probably the reason may be because the worms are drowned. The most insignificant insects and reptiles are of much more consequence, and have much more influence in the economy of nature, than the incurious are aware of; and are mighty in their effect, from their minuteness, which renders them less an object of attention; and from their numbers and fecundity. Earth-worms, though in appearance a small and despicable link in the chain of nature, yet, if lost, would make a lamentable chasm.

Gilbert White (1720–93), England

295. NOTHING IS USELESS

Among all the things that the Holy One, blessed be He, created in His Universe, He created nothing that is useless. He created the snail as a cure for scab, the fly as a cure for the sting of the wasp, the gnat as a cure for the bite of the serpent, the serpent as a cure for a sore, and the spider as a cure for the sting of a scorpion.

From the *Talmud* (6th century)

296. TO A YOUNG ATHLETE

Thing of a day! Such is man: a shadow in a dream.
Yet when god-given splendour visits him,
a bright radiance plays over him, and then how
sweet is life.
Pindar (c.518–c.438BCE), Greece

297. SUN AND STARS

The sun and stars that float in the open air
The apple-shaped Earth and we upon it,
surely the drift of them is something grand;
I do not know what it is except that it is grand, and
that it is happiness...
Walt Whitman (1819–92), from "Song of Myself", USA

298. THE MAGIC WORD

A song slumbers in all things
that lie dreaming on and on
and the world prepares to sing,
if you hit upon the magic word.
Joseph Freiherr von Eichendorff (1788–1857),
Germany

299. HEAVEN ON EARTH

Now that it is night,
you fetch in the washing
from outer space,

from the frozen garden
filmed like a kidney,
with a ghost in your mouth,

and everything you hold,
two floating shirts, a sheet,
ignores the law of gravity.

Only this morning,
the wren at her millinery,
making a baby's soft bonnet,

as we stopped by the spring,
watching the water
well up in the grass,

as if the world were teething.
It was heaven on earth
and it was only the morning.
Craig Raine (b.1944), England

300. MORNING AND EVENING

In the house made of dawn.
In the story made of dawn.
On the trail of dawn.
O, Talking God.
His feet, my feet, restore.
His limbs, my limbs, restore.
His body, my body, restore.
His voice, my voice, restore.
His plumes, my plumes, restore.
With beauty below him, with beauty below me.
With beauty around him, with beauty around me.
With pollen beautiful in his voice,
With pollen beautiful in my voice.
It is finished in beauty.
It is finished in beauty.
In the house of evening light.
From the story made of evening light.
On the trail of evening light.
Native American song, USA

301. HOLY THURSDAY

'Twas on a Holy Thursday, their innocent faces clean,
The children walking two and two, in red and blue
and green,
Grey-headed beadles walked before, with wands as
white as snow,
Till into the high dome of Paul's they like Thames'
waters flow.

O what a multitude they seemed, these flowers of
London town!
Seated in companies they sit with radiance all their
own.
The hum of multitudes was there, but multitudes of
lambs,
Thousands of little boys and girls raising their
innocent hands.

Now like a mighty wind they raise to heaven the
voice of song,
Or like harmonious thunderings the seats of heaven
among.
Beneath them sit the aged men, wise guardians of
the poor;
Then cherish pity, lest you drive an angel from your
door.

William Blake (1757–1827), England

302. THE SEA-CLIFF

Here come soaring
White gulls
Leisurely wheeling
In air over islands,
Sea pinks and salt grass,
Gannet and eider,
Curlew and cormorant
Each a differing
Pattern of ecstasy
Recurring at nodes
In an on-flowing current,
The perpetual species,
Repeated, renewed
By the will of joy
In eggs lodged safe
On perilous ledges.

Kathleen Raine (1908–2003), from
"The Moment", England

303. MEETING THE SUN

The smoke of my own breath,
Echoes, ripples, buzzed whispers, love-root, silk-
thread, crotch and vine,
My respiration and inspiration, the beating of my
heart, the passing of blood and air through my lungs,
The sniff of green leaves and dry leaves, and of the
shore and dark-colored sea-rocks, and of hay in the
barn,
The sound of the belched words of my voice loosed
to the eddies of the wind,
A few light kisses, a few embraces, a reaching around
of arms,
The play of shine and shade on the trees as the supple
boughs wag,
The delight alone or in the rush of the streets, or
along the fields and hill-sides,
The feeling of health, the full-noon trill, the song of me
rising from bed and meeting the sun.
Walt Whitman (1819–92), from "Song of Myself", USA

304. THE BIRTHRIGHT

We who were born
In country places,
Far from cities
And shifting faces,
We have a birthright
No man can sell,
And a secret joy
No man can tell.

For we are kindred
To lordly things,
The wild duck's flight
And the white owl's wings;
To pike and salmon,
To bull and horse,
The curlew's cry
And the smell of gorse.

Pride of trees,
Swiftness of streams,
Magic of frost
Have shaped our dreams:
No baser vision
Their spirit fills
Who walk by right
On the naked hills.

Eiluned Lewis (1900–79), Wales

305. TALL NETTLES

Tall nettles cover up, as they have done
These many springs, the rusty harrow,
    the plough
Long worn out, and the roller made of stone:
Only the elm butt tops the nettles now.

This corner of the farmyard I like most:
As well as any bloom upon a flower
I like the dust on the nettles, never lost
Except to prove the sweetness of a shower.
Edward Thomas (1878–1917), England

306. COSMIC LOVE

... love the universe as one's city, one's native
country, the beloved fatherland of every soul.
Simone Weil (1909–43), France

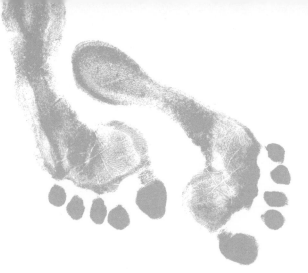

307. THE SACRED EARTH

Every part of this earth is sacred to my people.
Every shining pine needle, every sandy shore, every mist
in the dark wood, every clearing and humming
insect is holy in the memory and experience of my people...
We are part of the earth and it is part of us.
Chief Seathl (19th century), from "Chief Seathl's Testament", USA

308. LOVE IS MY KING

Love is and was my Lord and King,
    And in his presence I attend
    To hear the tidings of my friend,
Which every hour his couriers bring.

Love is and was my King and Lord,
    And will be, though as yet I keep
    Within his court on earth, and sleep
Encompassed by his faithful guard,

And hear at times a sentinel
    Who moves about from place to place,
    And whispers to the worlds of space,
In the deep night, that all is well.
Alfred, Lord Tennyson (1809–92), from "In
Memoriam", England

A WORLD OF PEACE

309. GRASS IN THE WIND

You who govern public affairs, what need have you
to employ punishments? Love virtue, and the people
will be virtuous. The virtues of a superior man are
like the wind; the virtues of a common man are like
the grass; the grass, when the wind passes over it,
bends.

Henry David Thoreau (1817–62), USA

310. HARVESTING

Let us aim to harvest peace.
Let us exhaust ourselves in ploughing
    the stony ground.

Modern prayer from Turkey

311. THE HALL OF PEACE

If anyone throws a stone,
>   may it be only to mark the limits
>   of the new foundations –

a great Hall of Peace in which we will all
>   give thanks to the Merciful Lord.

Modern prayer from Sri Lanka

312. THE HARMONIOUS KINGDOM

First there must be order and harmony within your
own mind. Then this order will spread to your
family, then to the community, and finally to your
entire kingdom. Only then can you have peace and
harmony.

Confucius (551–479 BCE), China

313. DIVINE SUNLIGHT

Abiding in Her magnificent shrine,
She shines Her protecting rays far
to the lands of the four corners,
Her radiant light bringing peace
everywhere under the heavens.
Inscription at the Ise Shrine, Japan
(referring to the sun goddess, Amaterasu)

THE ONE

314. WHO HAS SEEN THE WIND?

Who has seen the wind?
Neither I nor you:
But when the leaves hang trembling
The wind is passing through.

Who has seen the wind?
Neither you nor I:
But when the trees bow down their heads
The wind is passing by.
Christina Rossetti (1830–94), England

315. OMNIPRESENCE

Called or not called, God is always there.
Carl Jung (1875–1961), Switzerland

316. GOD'S NAME

And I say to mankind, Be not curious about God,
For I who am curious about each am not curious about
  God.
(No array of terms can say how much I am at peace
  about God and about death.)

I hear and behold God in every object, yet understand
  God not in the least,
Nor do I understand who there can be more wonderful
  than myself.
Why should I wish to see God better than this day?
I see something of God each hour of the twenty-four, and
  each moment then,
In the faces of men and women I see God, and in my own
  face in the glass,
I find letters from God dropped in the street, and every
  one is signed by God's name,
And I leave them where they are, for I know that
  wheresoever I go,
Others will punctually come for ever and ever.
Walt Whitman (1819–92), from "Song of Myself", USA

317. THE ALL-SEEING

However wild
He may be,
God can see,
God can save.
Anonymous (c.1370), from *Sir Gawain and the Green Knight*, England

318. A SHELTERING HEART

I asked for Peace – My sins arose,
And bound me close,
I could not find release.

I asked for Truth – My doubts came in,
And with their din
They wearied all my youth.

I asked for Love – My lovers failed,
And griefs assailed
Around, beneath, above.

I asked for Thee – And Thou didst come
To take me home
Within Thy heart to be.
D M Dolben (1848–67), England

319. LIGHT IN ALL CORNERS

God's wisdom must be regarded as the unique
source of all light upon Earth, even such feeble lights
as those which illumine the things of the world.
Simone Weil (1909–43), France

320. THE WORLD IN MY HAND

In his love he clothes us, enfolds and embraces us;
that tender love completely surrounds us, never to
leave us ... he showed me more, a little thing, the
size of a hazelnut on the palm of my hand, round
like a ball. I looked at it thoughtfully and wondered,
"What is this?" And the answer came, "It is all that
is made. ... It exists, both now and for ever, because
God loves it."
Julian of Norwich (c.1342–c.1413), England

321. GOD'S GOODNESS

"In you alone do I have all." Such
words are dear indeed unto the soul,
and very close to the will and goodness
of God. For he himself is eternity,
and has made us for himself alone,
has restored us by his blessed passion
and keeps us in his blessed love. And
all because he is goodness.
Julian of Norwich (c.1342–c.1413), England

322. THE LORD OF OPPOSITES

God is in the water of the lake; he is also in the
cracked bed of the lake when the lake has dried up.

God is in the abundant harvest; he is also in the
famine that occurs when the harvest fails.

God is in the lightning; he is also in the darkness
when the lightning has faded.
Mansur al-Hallaj (c.858–922), Persia

323. AWAKEN TO THE CHANGELESS

All is change in the world of the senses, but
changeless is the supreme Lord of Love. Meditate on
him, be absorbed in him, wake up from this dream of
separateness.

From the *Svetashvatara Upanishad* (600–300BCE),
India

324. STILLNESS AND UNION

When your mind, that may be wavering in the
contradictions of many scriptures, shall rest
unshaken in divine contemplation, then the goal
of union is yours.

From the *Bhagavad Gita* (1st–2nd century BCE), India

325. THE SELF AND THE LORD OF LOVE

Like oil in sesame seeds, like butter
in cream, like water in springs, like fire
in firesticks, so dwells the Lord of Love,
the Self, in the very depths of consciousness.
Realize him through truth and meditation.
From the *Svetashvatara Upanishad* (600–300BCE),
India

326. THE DEEPEST PERCEPTION

The more perfect and pure the powers of the
soul are, the more perfectly and comprehensively
they can receive the object of their perception,
embracing and experiencing a greater bliss, and
the more they become one with that which they
perceive, to such a degree indeed that the highest
power of the soul, which is free of all things and
which has nothing in common with anything else
at all, perceives nothing less than God himself in
the breadth and fullness of his being.
Meister Eckhart (1260–1328), Germany

327. OM

OM is the supreme symbol of the Lord.
OM is the whole. OM affirms; OM signals
the chanting of the hymns from the Vedas.
The priest begins with OM; spiritual teachers
and their students begin with OM.
The student who is established in OM
becomes united with the Lord of Love.
From the *Taittiriya Upanishad* (600–300BCE), India

328. ONE PLACE

Whether I fly with angels, fall with dust,
    Thy hands made both, and I am there:
    Thy power and love, my love and trust,
      Make one place everywhere.
George Herbert (1593–1633), from "The Temper",
England

329. LOVE'S FRAGRANCE

Make us, O Lord, flourish like pure, white lilies in the court of your house, giving forth the sweet fragrance of your love to all who pass.

Mozarabic Sacramentary (3rd century), Spain

330. OPENNESS

If it depended on me
    I would suppress
    All iron bars,
    All hedges,
    All walls.

If it depended on me
    Doors and windows –
    Except for rare moments
    When they must shield
    The King's secrets –
    Would remain open,
    Generously letting in
    The air and light and life!

Dom Hélder Câmara (1909–99), Brazil

331. THE CONVERSATION

Renew every day your conversation with God:
Do this even in preference to eating.
Think more often of God than you breathe.
Epictetus (c.55–c.155), Greece

332. ADAM'S SONG

I, I have strayed far from Your Keep
But I will return to Your Heart.

I, I have strayed far from Your Name
But I will return to Your Breath.

I, I have strayed far from Your Love
But I will return to Your Peace.
Jay Ramsay (b.1946), England

333. THE HEART'S REVELATION

I saw my Lord with the eye of my heart, and I said:
"Who art Thou?"
He said: "Thou."
Mansur al-Hallaj (858–922), Persia

334. INFINITE LOVE

At each beat of my heart I want, O my Beloved,
to renew my offering to you an infinite number of
times, until the shadows have disappeared and I can
tell you of my love face to face in eternity.
St Thérèse of Lisieux (1873–97), France

NEAR AND FAR HORIZONS

335. IMMORTALITY

My eyes want to flow into each other
like two neighbouring lakes.

To tell each other
everything they've seen.

My blood has many relatives.
They never visit.

But when they die,
my blood will inherit.

Yehuda Amichai (1924–2000), Israel

336. THE LAST HORIZON

As we climbed up the mountain and came to where I thought the horizon would be, it had disappeared – another horizon was waiting further on. I was disappointed, but also excited in an unfamiliar way. Each new level had revealed a new world. Against this perspective, death can be understood as the final horizon. Beyond there, the deepest well of your identity awaits you. In that well, you will behold the beauty and light of your eternal face.

John O'Donohue (1956–2008), Ireland

337. BETWEEN TWO NOTHINGS

Invisible before birth are all beings and after death invisible again. They are seen between two unseens. Why in this truth find sorrow?

From the *Bhagavad Gita* (1st–2nd century BCE), India

338. FACING MORTALITY

When you die, it will be not because you are sick, but because you were alive.

Seneca (c.4BCE–c.65CE), Rome

339. RESURRECTION IN TIME

I feel, looking back upon the past, that ... since I left school, I have had – like many, I suspect, of my War generation contemporaries – two quite separate lives ... The fact that, within ten years, I lost one world, and after a time rose again, as it were, from spiritual death to find another, seems to me one of the strongest arguments against suicide that life can provide ... resurrection is possible within our limited span of earthly time.

Vera Brittain (1893–1970), England

340. THE BEETLE'S EGG

Every one has heard the story which has gone the rounds of New England, of a strong and beautiful bug which came out of the dry leaf of an old table of apple-tree wood, which had stood in a farmer's kitchen for sixty years, first in Connecticut, and afterward in Massachusetts – from an egg deposited in the living tree many years earlier still, as appeared by counting the annual layers beyond it; which was heard gnawing out for several weeks, hatched perchance by the heat of an urn. Who does not feel his faith in a resurrection and immortality strengthened by hearing of this?

Henry David Thoreau (1817–62), USA

341. THE UNKNOWN

Life is a great surprise. I do not see why death should not be an even greater one.

Vladimir Nabokov (1899–1977), USA

342. NIGHT JOURNEY

Dying is a wild night and a new road.
Emily Dickinson (1830–86), USA

343. THE PARTING

When the parting suddenly flings wide forever
The unknown distance, in a little while,
I'll remember everything by name, by the quiver
Of their wise and bashful smile.

I shall put my dead face on with a silence free
Of joy and of pain evermore,
And dawn will trail like a child after me
To play with shells on the shore.
Yocheved Bat-Miriam (1901–79), born in Russia,
settled in Palestine

344. SOUL AND BODY

The spirit looks upon the dust
That fastened it so long
With indignation,
As a Bird
Defrauded of its song.
Emily Dickinson (1830–86), USA

345. THE SPAN OF LIFE

Is there not a certain satisfaction in the fact that
natural limits are set to the life of the individual,
so that at the conclusion it may appear as a work
of art?
Albert Einstein (1879–1955), Germany/USA

346. IMPOSSIBILITY

Thou in me and I in thee. Death! what is death?
There is no death: *in thee* it is impossible, absurd.
Mark Rutherford (1829–1913), England

347. THE FLIGHT OF THE SOUL

Pure, goodly soul, how long will you journey on?
You are the King's falcon. Fly back toward the
Emperor's whistle!
Jalal al-Din Rumi (1207–73), Persia

348. WHEN THE TIME COMES

When the time comes, I will know that death is a
homecoming,

    not a wrench that leaves a bruise on my spirit.

Death is not the shadow but the light beyond the
shadow.

My spirit will return to its resting place
    in a long, slow glide toward peace.
Modern meditation from Orkney, Scotland

349. LEAVETAKING

My delight in death
exceeds the pleasure of a merchant
who makes a vast fortune,
or a victorious war god,
or a sage in total trance.
Like a traveller taking to the road,
I will leave this world and return home ...
My life is over and my karma is done with ...
I am approaching the ground of primal perfection.

Longchenpa (1308–64), Tibet

350. THE TRIUMPH OF LIFE

And death shall have no dominion.
Dead men naked they shall be one
With the man in the wind and the west moon;
When their bones are picked clean and the clean
bones gone,
They shall have stars at elbow and foot;
Though they go mad they shall be sane,
Though they sink through the sea they shall rise
again;
Though lovers be lost love shall not;
And death shall have no dominion.
Dylan Thomas (1914–53), from "And death shall have
no dominion", Wales

351. THE EMPTY CHAMBER

Go sweep the chamber of your heart. Make it ready
to be the dwelling-place of the Beloved. When you
depart, He will enter it. In you, empty of yourself, He
will display all his beauty.
Shabistari (1288–1340), Iran

352. THE ETERNAL NOW

Not with thoughts of your mind, but in the believing
sweetness of your heart, you snap the link and open
the golden door and disappear into the bright room,
the everlasting ecstasy, eternal Now.

Jack Kerouac (1923–69), USA

353. DAWN

O Night and Dark,
O huddled sullen clouds,
Light enters in the sky
Whitens.
Christ comes! Depart! Depart!

The mist sheers apart,
Cleft by the sun's spear.
Colour comes back to things
From his bright face.

Prudentius (c.348–c.410), from
"At a beautiful dawn, after bad weather", Spain

354. THE DREAM

For the first four years after she died, I felt like an orphan. Then one night she came to me in a dream, and from that moment on, I no longer felt her death as a loss. I understood that she had never died, that my sorrow was based on an illusion. ... The reality of my mother was beyond birth or death. She did not exist because of birth, nor cease to exist because of death. I saw that being and non-being are not separate. ... Being able to see my mother in my dream, I realized that I could see my mother everywhere.

Thich Nhat Hanh (b.1926), Vietnam

355. SHE

I think the dead are tender. Shall we kiss? –
My lady laughs, delighting in what is.
If she but sighs, a bird puts out its tongue.
She makes space lonely with a lovely song.
She lilts a low soft language, and I hear
Down long sea-chambers of the inner ear.

We sing together; we sing mouth to mouth.
The garden is a river flowing south.
She cries out loud the soul's own secret joy;
She dances, and the ground bears her away.
She knows the speech of light, and makes it plain
A lively thing can come to life again.

I feel her presence in the common day,
In that slow walk that widens every eye.
She moves as water moves, and comes to me,
Stayed by what was, and pulled by what would be.
Theodore Roethke (1908–63), USA

356. THE IMPRISONED SOUL

At the last, tenderly,
From the walls of the powerful, fortressed house,
From the clasp of the knitted locks – from the keep
    of the well-closed doors,
Let me be wafted.

Let me glide noiselessly forth;
With the key of softness unlock the locks –
    with a whisper
Set ope the doors, O soul!
Walt Whitman (1819–92), USA

357. HIDDEN TREASURE

The kingdom of heaven is like treasure hidden in a
field, which someone found and hid; then in his joy
he goes and sells all that he has and buys that field.
Matthew 13:44

358. THE FIRST STAGE

The grave is the first stage of the journey into
eternity.

From the *Hadith* (c.7th century), the spoken Islamic
tradition attributed to the Prophet Muhammad

359. A PLACE TO REST

Thou art the true peace of the heart, Thou art its
only rest; out of Thee all things are full of trouble
and difficulty. In this peace, that is, in Thee, the one
sovereign eternal Good, I will sleep and take my rest.
Amen.

Thomas à Kempis (1380–1471), Germany

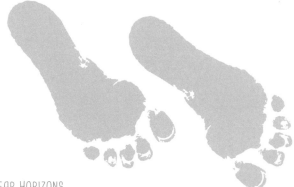

ETERNITY

360. THE PRESENT MOMENT

In eternity there is indeed
    something true and sublime.
But all these times and places
    and occasions are now and here.
God himself culminates in the
    present moment, and will
    never be more divine in the
    lapse of all the ages.
Henry David Thoreau (1817–62), USA

361. DISSOLUTION

We,
Like parted drops of rain
Swelling till they melt and run,
Shall be all absorbed
Again –

Melting,
Flowing into one.
Christopher Pearse Cranch (1813–92), USA

362. MIST AND SKY

The purity men love is like the mists which envelop the earth, and not like the azure ether beyond.

Henry David Thoreau (1817–62), USA

363. TIME'S PLACE

Time of its own power cooks all beings within itself. No-one, however, knows that in which Time itself is being cooked.

From the *Mahabharata* (6th century BCE), India

364. LEGACY

Nothing that is can dissolve into nothingness! In all that lives the Eternal Force works on: remain, rejoicing, in Being! Being is eternal; for laws preserve the living treasures with which the universe has adorned itself.

Johann Wolfgang von Goethe (1749–1832), Germany

365. A QUESTION OF TIME

To every one of us there must come a time when the whole universe will be found to have been a dream, when we find the soul is infinitely better than its surroundings. It is only a question of time, and time is nothing in the infinite.

Shirdi Sai Baba (1838–1918), India

ACKNOWLEDGEMENTS

Acknowledgements have been listed by quotation number.

3, 24, 217, 240 from COLLECTED POEMS OF WALLACE STEVENS by Wallace Stevens, copyright © 1954 by Wallace Stevens and renewed 1982 by Holly Stevens (Faber & Faber, 1955). Reprinted by permission of the publishers and Alfred A. Knopf, a division of Random House, Inc. US; **4** from THE RUBAIYAT by Jalal al-Din Rumi, translated by Azima Medita Kolin and Maryam Mafi, translation copyright © Maryam Mafi and Azima Medita Kolin, 1999 (Thorsons, an imprint of HarperCollins); **5, 26, 326** from SELECTED WRITINGS by Meister Eckhart, translated by Oliver Davies, copyright © Oliver Davies, 1994. Reproduced by permission of Penguin Books Ltd; **10, 155, 352** from THE SCRIPTURE OF THE GOLDEN ETERNITY by Jack Kerouac (City Lights, 1994); **11, 43, 72, 106, 112, 156** from BUDDHA'S LITTLE INSTRUCTION BOOK by Jack Kornfield (Rider, 1996). Reprinted by permission of the Random House Group Ltd, UK; **12, 54, 275, 364** from GOETHE: SELECTED VERSE, translated by David Luke, copyright © David Luke, 1964 (Penguin Classics); **14** from LIFE SENTENCE: SELECTED POEMS by Nina Cassian, translated by Eva Feiler and Nina Cassian, edited by William Jay Smith. Copyright © 1990 by Nina Cassian. Published by Anvil Press

Poetry in 1990. Reprinted by permission of Anvil Press and W.W. Norton and Company, Inc.; **16, 39, 47, 194, 324** from THE BHAGAVAD GITA, translated by Juan Mascaro, copyright © Juan Mascaro, 1962. Reproduced by permission of Penguin Books Ltd; **19, 249, 338** from THE SPIRITUAL TEACHINGS OF SENECA by Mark Forstater and Victoria Rodin (Hodder Mobius, 2001). Reprinted by permission of Hodder and Stoughton Ltd, London, and Penguin Putnam, New York; **22** from the TAO TE CHING by Lao Tzu, 1993, translated by Lombardo and Addiss. Reprinted by permission of Hackett Publishing Company Inc. All rights reserved; **25** from A GOLDEN TREASURY OF CHINESE POETRY, edited by John Deeney, translated by John Turner, Renditions Books, Hong Kong Research Centre for Translation of the Chinese University of Hong Kong, 1997, p.101. Reprinted by permission of the publishers; **30** translated by Tom Lowenstein from HAIKU INSPIRATIONS; **33, 38, 48, 54, 67, 82, 90, 91, 92, 98, 101, 162, 165, 168, 170, 172, 186, 184, 196, 197, 214, 225, 220, 228, 244, 276, 279, 310, 311** translations copyright © Duncan Baird Publishers, London, 2002; **42, 45, 259** from THE SPIRITUAL TEACHINGS OF MARCUS AURELIUS by Mark Forstater 2001. Reprinted by permission of Hodder and Stoughton Ltd; **44, 120** from MAGNIFICENT ONE: SELECTIONS FROM RUMI'S DIVAN-I KEBIR by Jalal al-Din Rumi, translated by Nevit Oguz Ergin (Larson Publications, 1993); **46, 216** from BREATHING TRUTH: RUMI QUOTATIONS by Muriel Maufroy (Blue Dolphin Publishing, 1997); **49, 149, 154** from THE

WISDOM OF THE TIBETAN LAMAS by Shantideva, copyright ©
Timothy Freke (Godsfield Press, 1999). Reprinted by
permission of David & Charles Ltd, London; **53** from THE
KORAN INTERPRETED by A J Arberry, copyright © A J Arberry,
1942. Reprinted by permission of HarperCollins Publishers
Ltd; **64** from INTRODUCING BUDDHA, translation copyright ©
Jane Hope (Icon Books Ltd, 1999); **69, 354** from THE HEART
OF THE BUDDHA'S TEACHING (1998) by Thich Nhat Hanh with
permission of Parallax Press, Berkeley, California. Paperback
edition, 1999, Broadway Books, New York; **73** from THE HAW
LANTERN by Seamus Heaney (Faber & Faber, 1987). Reprinted
by permission of the publishers and Farrar, Straus & Giroux,
New York; **76, 108** from THE DIARY OF A YOUNG GIRL by Anne
Frank, translated by Susan Massotty and Euan Cameron,
edited by Otto H Frank and Miriam Pressler (Penguin Books,
2000); **79** from THE SELECTED POEMS OF TOMAS
TRANSTRÖMER, translated by Robin Fulton (Bloodaxe Books,
1997). Reprinted by permission of the publishers; **80** from LE
PARTI PRIS DES CHOSES by Francis Ponge, edited and
translated by Margaret Guiton (Editions Gallimard, 1942).
Reprinted by permission of Red Dust, New York, and Wake
Forest University Press, New York; **87** from THE SPIRIT LEVEL
by Seamus Heaney (Faber & Faber, 1996). Reprinted by
permission of the publishers and Farrar, Straus & Giroux, New
York; **90** from WILD WAYS: ZEN POEMS OF IKKYU, translated
by John Stevens, copyright © 1995. Reprinted by permission
of Shambhala Publications, Inc., Boston, www.shambhala.

com; **96, 256** from DESERT WISDOM: SAYINGS FROM THE DESERT FATHERS by Henri J M Nonwen and Yushi Nomura, copyright © 1982, 2001 (Orbis Books, New York). Reprinted by permission of the publishers; **102, 363** from MAHABHARATA translated by William Buck. Copyright © 1973 The Regents of the University of California, published by University of California Press. Reprinted with permission of the publishers; **104, 141** from COLLECTED POEMS: 1945–1990 by R S Thomas (Orion Paperbacks, 2000). Reprinted by permission of the publishers; **119, 288** from SONNETS TO ORPHEUS (II, vi, and I,iv), adaptation copyright © Robert Saxton, 2002; **121** translated from Gujarati by Sitanshu Yashashchandra, from THE OXFORD ANTHOLOGY OF MODERN INDIAN POETRY (Oxford University Press, 1997); **123, 332** from KINGDOM OF THE EDGE: POEMS FOR THE SPIRIT by Jay Ramsay (Element Books Ltd, 1999). Reprinted by permission of Chrysalis Books Plc, UK; **132** from BURNING GIRAFFES: MODERN AND CONTEMPORARY JAPANESE POETRY, translated by James Hirkup (University of Salzburg Press, 1996); **133** from COLLECTED POEMS: 1909–1939, VOLUME 1 by William Carlos Williams, copyright © New Directions Corp., 1938 (Carcanet Press, 2000). Reprinted by permission of New Directions Publishing Corp., New York, and Carcanet Press Ltd, Manchester; **134, 139, 140, 192, 219, 264, 286, 357** The Scripture quotations contained herein are from the New Revised Standard Version Bible, copyright © 1989 by the Division of Christian Education of the National

Council of the Churches of Christ in the USA, and are used by permission. All rights reserved; **135, 167, 266** from THE VISION: REFLECTIONS ON THE WAY OF THE SOUL by Kahlil Gibran, translated by Juan R I Cole translation copyright © Juan R I Cole, 1997. Reproduced by permission of Penguin Books Ltd; **137** from ANOTHER DAY: PRAYERS OF THE HUMAN FAMILY, compiled and edited by John Carden, copyright © SPCK, London, 1986. Reprinted by permission of the publishers; **145, 298** translation copyright © Hanne Bewernick, 2002; **169, 173** from RUMI: DAYLIGHT, translated by Camille and Kabir Helminski, copyright © Camille and Kabir Helminski, 1994 (Shambhala). Reprinted by permission of Shambhala Publications, Inc., Boston, www.shambhala.com; **178, 229, 235, 238** from COLLECTED POEMS by Anne Ridler (Carcanet Press Ltd, 1994). Reprinted by permission of the publishers; **179** from POEMS 1963–1983 by Michael Longley published by Secker & Warburg. Reprinted by permission of Jonathan Cape, a division of the Random House Group Ltd, London; **195** from NORTH by Seamus Heaney (Faber & Faber, 1996). Reprinted by permission of the publishers and Farrar, Straus & Giroux, New York; **204** from THE SOVEREIGNTY OF GOOD by Iris Murdoch, copyright © 1971 Iris Murdoch (Routledge, imprint of Taylor and Francis Group). Reprinted by permission of the publishers; **205** from THE PROPHET by Kahlil Gibran, copyright © 1923 by Kahlil Gibran and renewed 1951 by Administrators C.T.A. of Kahlil Gibran Estate and Mary G Gibran (Heinemann, 1993). Reproduced by permission of

Alfred A Knopf, a division of Random House, Inc., USA, and Gibran National Committee, P.O. Box 116–5375, Beirut, Lebanon. Phone & Fax: (+961–1) 396916; email: k.gibran@cyberia.net.lb; **209** from THE CHINE by Mimi Khalvati (Carcanet Press Ltd, 2002). Reprinted by permission of the publishers; **210** from COMPLETE POEMS 1904–1962, by e e cummings, edited by George J Firmage, copyright © 1991 by the Trustees for the E.E. Cummings Trust and George James Firmage (Liveright, 1994). Reprinted by permission of W W Norton & Company, London; **211** from THE INK DARK MOON by Jane Hirschfield and Mariko Aratani, copyright © Jane Hirschfield and Mariko Aratani, 1990 (Vintage Classics, 1990). Reprinted by permission of Vintage Books, a division of Random House, Inc., New York; **212** from the "Sian Bhuddha" in THE LITTLE BOOK OF CELTIC BLESSINGS, compiled by Caitlin Matthews, copyright © Caitlin Matthews, 1994 (Element Books Ltd). Reprinted by permission of HarperCollins Publishers Ltd, London; **223** from DANTE'S INFERNO CANTO V translated by John D Sinclair, published by Bodley Head. Used by permission of The Random House Group Limited; **230, 343** from HEBREW LOVE POEMS edited by David L Gross, copyright © David L Gross, 1995. Reprinted by permission of Hippo Crene Books; **233** from SELECTED POEMS by Pauline Stainer (Bloodaxe Books). Reprinted by permission of the publishers; **234** from COLLECTED POEMS by Derek Mahon, 1999. Reprinted by permission of the author and The Gallery Press, County Meath, Loughcrew, Oldcastle,

Ireland; **236** from AN ANTHOLOGY OF VIETNAMESE POEMS, edited and translated by Huynsh Sash Thong (Yale University Press, 1996); **241** from THE EYES by Antonio Machado, adaptation by Don Paterson (Faber & Faber, 1999). Reprinted by permission of the publishers; **248, 322** from 366 READINGS FROM ISLAM edited by Robert van de Weyer. Reprinted by permission of John Hunt Publishing Ltd; **253** from THE POCKET RUMI READER, copyright © Kabir Helminski, 2001 (Shambhala). Reprinted by permission of Shambhala Publications, Inc., Boston,www.shambhala.com; **258** from PLATO: SYMPOSIUM (1986) and PHAEDERUS (2000), translated by Tom Griffith, translation copyright © Tom Griffith, 1986 (Everyman's Library). Reprinted by permission of the author; **269** from BIRDS OF HEAVEN by Ben Okri, copyright © Ben Okri (Phoenix House and Orion). Reprinted by permission of David Godwin Associates, London; **270** from A DIARY OF PRIVATE PRAYER by John Baillie, copyright © 1949 by Charles Scribner's Sons and renewed 1977 by Ian Fowler Baillie (Simon & Schuster, 1996). Reprinted by permission of Scribner, Inc., and Oxford University Press; **273, 320, 321** from REVELATIONS OF DIVINE LOVE by Julian of Norwich, translated by Elizabeth Spearing, translation copyright © Elizabeth Spearing, 1998 (Penguin Classics). Reproduced by permission of Penguin Books Ltd; **293** from FROM DARKNESS TO LIGHT (POEMS AND PARABLES) by Jiddu Krishnamurti, copyright © Krishnamurti Foundation of America (Victor Gollancz, 1981); **299** from COLLECTED POEMS 1978–1998 by

Craig Raine (Picador, 2000). Reprinted by permission of David Godwin Associates, London; **302** from THE COLLECTED POEMS OF KATHLEEN RAINE, Golgonooza Press, Ipswich, 2000. Copyright © Kathleen Raine 2000. Reprinted by permission of Golgonooza Press (UK) and Counterpoint Press (US), a member of Perseus Books, L.L.C.; **304** Reprinted by permission of Mrs Katrina Burnett, copyright © Mrs Katrina Burnett (The Estate of Eiluned Lewis); **307** from THE GREAT CHIEF SENDS WORD. Distributed by One Village, Chalbury, OX7 35Q; **335** from SELECTED POEMS by Yehuda Amichai (Faber & Faber, 2000). Reprinted by permission of the publishers; **336** from ANAM CARA: SPIRITUAL WISDOM FROM THE CELTIC FAITH by John O'Donohue (Bantam Press). Copyright © 1997 by John O'Donohue. Reprinted by permission of Transworld Publishers, a division of the Random House Group Ltd, London and HarperCollins Publishers Inc. (US); **339** from TESTAMENT OF YOUTH by Vera Brittain (Virago Press, 1992). Reprinted by permission of her literary executors, Mark Bostridge and Rebecca Williams, and Victor Gollancz Ltd; **343** from HEBREW LOVE POEMS, edited by David L Gross. Copyright © David L Gross 1995. Reprinted by permission of Hippo Crene Books, New York; **350** from THE COLLECTED POEMS 1934–1953 by Dylan Thomas (Orion Paperbacks, 2000). Reprinted by permission of David Higham Associates, London; **355** from COLLECTED POEMS by Theodore Roethke (Bantam Dell Publishing, 1978). Reprinted by kind permission of the publishers.

The publishers have made every effort to contact copyright holders. We should like to apologize for any errors or omissions, which we will endeavour to rectify in future printings of this book.

The publishers would like to thank Hanne Bewernick, Catherine Bradley and Tony Allan for their advice on the selection of quotations for this book.

WATKINS
Sharing Wisdom Since 1893

The story of Watkins began in 1893, when scholar of esotericism John Watkins founded our bookshop, inspired by the lament of his friend and teacher Madame Blavatsky that there was nowhere in London to buy books on mysticism, occultism or metaphysics. That moment marked the birth of Watkins, soon to become the publisher of many of the leading lights of spiritual literature, including Carl Jung, Rudolf Steiner, Alice Bailey and Chögyam Trungpa.

Today, the passion at Watkins Publishing for vigorous questioning is still resolute. Our stimulating and groundbreaking list ranges from ancient traditions and complementary medicine to the latest ideas about personal development, holistic wellbeing and consciousness exploration. We remain at the cutting edge, committed to publishing books that change lives.

DISCOVER MORE AT:

www.watkinspublishing.com

Read our blog

Watch and listen to
our authors in action

Sign up to
our mailing list

We celebrate conscious, passionate, wise and happy living.
Be part of that community by visiting

 /watkinspublishing    @watkinswisdom
    /watkinsbooks   @watkinswisdom